The Loving Person

The Loving Person

Person and Ethics

NINA KARIN MONSEN

RESOURCE *Publications* • Eugene, Oregon

THE LOVING PERSON
Person and Ethics

Copyright © 2021 Nina Karin Monsen. All rights reserved. Except for brief quotations in critical publications or reviews, no part of this book may be reproduced in any manner without prior written permission from the publisher. Write: Permissions, Wipf and Stock Publishers, 199 W. 8th Ave., Suite 3, Eugene, OR 97401.

Resource Publications
An Imprint of Wipf and Stock Publishers
199 W. 8th Ave., Suite 3
Eugene, OR 97401

www.wipfandstock.com

PAPERBACK ISBN: 978-1-6667-0658-1
HARDCOVER ISBN: 978-1-6667-0659-8
EBOOK ISBN: 978-1-6667-0660-4

10/11/21

In memory of my father, Peter Monsen, 1910–74

...The human being sits at the doorway to the poetry,
she came here once from an unknown place.
Walking through whip and plague and fire
and desert sand,
Followed by evil and blood and
on to circus joy and desolate scream.
But vision and dream she also carried
flying like birdsong over alp and heath,
as a trembling stubborn song about light
surrounding frozen spring and dead houses
The journey of men oddly distorted
round what we call God's beautiful world.
Although we can also tell
and cling to it:
that all that is god-like and great
and light the fires
this has man done.
She has counted star's paths and years
where they silently pass through endless space.
She sits by instrument and service
herself she is just a moment.
Herself she is just a gust in the wind,
a birth cry and a furrowed cheek,
—NILS FERLIN (SWEDISH AUTHOR, 1898–1961),
AT THE DOORWAY TO THE POETRY

Contents

Preface to the American edition		ix
Preface to the Norwegian edition		xi
Front Matter Endnotes		xiv
Chapter I	Terminology	1
Chapter II	Towards the Person	10
Chapter III	Inner Reality	26
Chapter IV	Interpersonal Room	35
Chapter V	Personal Reality	60
Chapter VI	Personalizing Processes	73
Chapter VII	Housekeeping of the Person	93
Chapter VIII	Person and Society	115
Recommended Literature		137
Chapter Endnotes		138

Preface to the American edition

I AM VERY PLEASED that my book, *The Loving Person: Person and Ethics*, is being published in USA. The book was written in the 1980s and has lived with me through many editions and publishers, lectures and speeches in many different settings. It has been used as books for study, especially in colleges for the field of health education. For a while people even called me the nurses' philosopher. The book is a hand to hold on to, one reader told me. The same do I feel about many books in my library, I think of them as friends who comfort me. This love of books of hope, trust and goodness, has followed me in my lifelong reading and still does.

    I am grateful that I had the opportunity to read all those lovely books that I am referring to in my book. There are many more authors that I could have mentioned. One is Martin Luther King who studied at Boston School of Theology. This university had a professorship in personalism for many years. I met some of the personalists there in 1990, when I stayed in Boston for three months. Other philosophers I could have mentioned are Pope Johannes II and his follower Joseph Ratzinger.

    I grew up in an anti-Christian family. I was in many years a stranger to Christian congregations, knowing very little of norms and rules. I left the Church (State Church) when I was 19 years old. But even as a child I did have a clear vision of the existence of God as a person, the most natural recipient of all thoughts. I have always been searching for the truth, without truth, thinking and philosophy is a mere game.

    I studied mostly analytical philosophy, for one year also mathematical logic, and I was fascinated by the complicated structures. But without the person and the yearning for meaning, communication and understanding of another human being, the structures take one outside the personal reality. There is where I want to be.

    In 2009 I received The prize of Free Speech in Norway (from the Fritt Ord Foundation, Oslo) for my long engagement in the debate about the development in modern societies (since the 1970s). The committee honored me for my writings about freedom and dignity for both men and women, women as persons, sexuality, love and moral philosophy.

In 2013 I was accepted as a member of the Catholic Church. To me it was a natural choice and also followed logically from my work about the person in many years. I have a master degree in Philosophy (Oslo University), have written 22 books, both fiction and non-fiction, a hundreds of articles. For my CV see nina.karin.monsen@worldpress.com. I am also writing short notes on Facebook almost every day, and am blessed with many likes and almost 5000 friends.

Nina Karin Monsen

Preface to the Norwegian edition

IN THE WORDS OF a poem it is said:
"New organs of perception come into being as a result of need,
Therefore, O man, increase your need,
So, that you may increase your perception."[1]

This book is written to challenge and encourage people to increase their need to be a person, so that as many as possibly can become sensitive enough to catch sight of the personal and develop courage to live in an ethical reality.

The Loving Person is a book about philosophy of life. It concerns the human existence, responsibilities and goals and describes what it means to be a human being, the immanent human being.

The thoughts in this book are inspired by several philosophers and poets, all part of an Existentialist, Personalist, and Humanist philosophical tradition, both with and without religious convictions. The ideas and thoughts presented here are descriptive of human reality and express my own experience.

The thoughts that have inspired me come from some of the great philosophers and poets. Let me here mention only one; the French philosopher *Emmanuel Mounier* (1905—1950). Mounier was an intellectual spirit in French cultural life, first and foremost through the monthly magazine, "Esprit," which he started in 1933, ran until his death. It still exists. Dubbed the "Spirit of the French Resistance," Mounier also gained importance and relevance through his actions during the Second World War.

Mounier is an example of a philosopher that integrated emotion and intellect, his thoughts should never run wild and emotions should always be anchored in the conscious mind and in wisdom. As an active catholic that was natural to him. His truthful passionate thinking, or thoughtful sensitivity, is a lesson to everybody. His message was that reality, meaning, and true understanding presuppose love and communication. He shows the possibility of man, the authentic human being: the person.[2]

The Loving Person is written in the spirit of Mounier, with a starting point that only a philosophy of love can offer. But it is not a review of the philosophy of Mounier, or an analysis of his thoughts.

The thoughts presented here can be understood from many different aspects. In one sense, it is one *philosophy*, one system of thought and a separate philosophical school, personalism.[3]

It is also a *"method"* that guides people towards a more profound life experience, a clearer understanding of the meaning of life, and developing and enhance their personal growth.

This philosophy is therefore also *a way of life*. Primarily that means an existence where a fundamental ethical dimension, an ethical experience, is essential. Becoming a person becomes a crusade, a crusade to shape reality and goodness, to promote communication and true fellowship.

My reasons for writing this book are not based on Christian background. However, at least part of the motivation for writing it is based on experiences of spirit, or experiences of values, that can cause others to identify as Christian. I wish that spiritual and intellectual thoughts and experiences shall influence me and others without resulting in any rigid debate or arguments, without evoking discussions, conflicts, and battles about who possesses the "true" faith. The person must always come first. And persons invite to a conversation. Therefore, I invite the reader first and foremost to a dialog on what it means to be human.

It is likely that some will criticize me for being optimistic on behalf of humanity. They will point out that people are evil and act with unimaginable brutality and indifference. To that I would answer that countless people act with goodness; it is because there is more good than evil in the world that the world still exists. And, maintain that no one is so evil that they have no possibility for goodness within.

The two first chapters are first and foremost a presentation of personalism, its concepts and their content. The next two chapters describe those universal life experiences that form the foundation for this philosophy. The fifth chapter is a synthesis of these essential life experiences. Chapter six defines the personal as form of life and process. The seventh chapter expands on the inherent value of the ethical human: the loving person. That final chapter is a general critique of society from a personalist point of view.

I have attempted to write each of the various chapters as a whole. As a result, it has been necessary to be somewhat repetitive, and yet, at times, perhaps not always thorough enough. While writing, I often experienced the danger of presenting a theme as either too complex or too banal. One can easily fall into both pitfalls when writing about philosophies of life and thoughts about people. That 'goes with the territory' so to speak.

Regardless, it has been a pleasure and a joy to write about something that strikes me as so important and so fundamental.

Nina Karin Monsen
Oslo May 1987

Front Matter Endnotes

1. Indries Shah: *Tales of the Dervishes*, (New York Penguin Compass, 1993) 197
2. Jean Conilh, *Emmanuel Mounier Sa vie, son oeuvre avec un exposé de sa philosophie,* (Paris, Presses Universitaires de France, 1966)
3. The terms 'Personalist' and "personalism" were first used in the 1860s in the United States by Walt Whitman and Bronson Alcott, in 1803 in France by Charles Renouvier, and in 1906 in Germany by William Stern. However, Personalist thinking can be traced back in the history of philosophy to Heracles (536–470 BC). Many of the greatest thinkers in the history of philosophy have been impressed by personalistic ideas. In newer times the Danish philosopher Søren Kierkegaard (1813–1855) clearly underlined the importance of the personal in and for human understanding.

Chapter I

Terminology

LIMITING LANGUAGE CAN BE useful. It makes one sharpen the conscious mind about nuances that words have, and reveal the insights and knowledge that language holds. At least, preparing language for a theme is especially important when the subject is the human being and the view of man. To better understand the distinctive qualities and destiny of the human being, we need to have the tools, concepts well in hand.

The use of the term PERSON in this book is of vital importance. It is a philosophical term, and as such, will be used by me approximately as personalism explains it. This is made complicated by the fact that the term often is used differently in our daily language, and sometimes against the philosophical meaning. Another complication is the fact that the words individual, human being, and person are used as synonyms and individual, human and personal often mean the same. But in Norwegian language and culture there is also stored the same insight that personalism builds on and develops.

For this reasons, it is necessary to clarify the use of these philosophical terms: person, personal, and personality as opposed to the terms individual, and individuality, human and humane. In this chapter, I will take a look at the use of these words in daily language unlike personalism.

A Brief History of the Concept of the Person

It is supposed that the word *persona* comes from Latin, where it originally was the term for the mask of tragedy that actors used in the Roman Theater. This mask was a symbol for forefathers, family, and ancestors in past, present, and future, adding a dimension of eternity to society. It is probably that the Romans borrowed this word from the Etruscans who in turn had taken it from the Greeks.

In the Roman law the concept of person is a distinctive category. Roman Legislation distinguished between two categories: things and persons. The concept of the person had a particular value in Roman culture. With the concept comes increased freedom in society, first within the family for the sons, then for commoners, the plebeians. Anyone who could appear in court was considered a person, and that added value to their general status.

The dignity of the person was also strengthened by the infusion of different first names from one generation to another, as is common today. This served to emphasize the individuality of each separate being.

Because Roman law had a personal structure, all people under its jurisdiction were considered free except for the slaves. The free man was a *person* and had a *personality*. This dignity was further developed to include the immortal soul during the expansion of Christianity. As a natural result, a moral dimension was added to the person; each person was independent, autonomous, and responsible. More recently a psychological dimension has been added, the person is the modern human being.

When Christianity was introduced into Roman society, the concept of individual liberty and an immortal soul, which no one else could own, was strengthened. The view of the human being grew from that of a being with legal rights and ethical responsibilities to a being that was part of the divine.

The development in philosophy added an even more important step, probably from *Johann Gottlieb Fichte* (1762–1814). The Person, the self, the I or whatever one chooses to call him or her, became a separate category, a fundamental category of thought. In this way the person also became a requirement for consciousness, science, and pure reason.

In our society we understand the concept of person first and foremost through the American "Declaration of the Rights of Man" and from the French Revolution. The Norwegian Constitution is based on a similar view of humanity. Most of the revolutions of the past few centuries can be viewed as demands to affirm rights for increasingly large numbers of people to be treated as persons, not least of all in a legal and a political context.

Marcel Mauss describes this development as one "From a simple masquerade to the mask, from a role to a person, to a name, an individual; from the latter to a being with metaphysical and moral value; from a moral consciousness to a sacred being; from the last to a fundamental category of thought and action, and the course is accomplished."[1]

To deny the person and the personal can be viewed as an attempt to reverse developments by a couple of thousand years and to act against the fundamental ideas that have guided the development of European culture.

Norwegian Everyday Speech

According to Norwegian dictionary of synonyms Person means: face, element, figure, apparition, gestalt, head, individual, character, body, man, human being, Master Urian, pappenheimer, persona, personage, personality, public, (not a mother's) soul, creature, shape, subject, type, being, chap. *Personal* is uses as: at one's own expense, individual, original, independent, subjective, one's own, one's own hand, one's own part, owner, in one's high person, self, in the flesh, by personal inspection, direct, intimate, confidential, private, face to face, rude, aggressive, partial, hurting, offensive, impudent. *Personality* means: distinctive, individuality, character, inclination, mood, psyche, self, mind, style, distinctive, spirit, authority, the only one, man, personality, size, spiritual leader.

While *individual* may mean: the only one, specimen, element, single, human being, specimen, subject, special. *Individuality* means personal, special, unique, distinct, mind.

The *human being* may mean: Homo Sapiens, earthbound, living soul, mother's soul, fellow wanderer, citizen of the world, individual, person. *Humane* means: human, earthly, soft. *Humanity* means: human, compassion. [2]

As anyone can see, language is an abundance of words. Additionally, some usages of the words do not appear in dictionaries. A concept that I will use a lot is mass/man/woman, is not mentioned in this dictionary.

Personalist Language Usage

Let me repeat that the philosophical insights considered is not gripped from thin air. They are our inheritance from Western civilization and are reflected in both our culture and our language.

To follow personalist thinking, we must establish clear boundaries between the concepts. Not at least because it is interesting to get a map of values and consequences each separate concept is loaded with and point to. It is vitally important to acknowledge the person and the personal as a third dimension that transcends both the individual and the collective.

A. The term *person* is the most important term used in my philosophical context, and the understanding of this term is decisive. Person, personality and personal are clearly determinations of quality. The terms relate to inner qualities and interpersonal relationships, they are comparative and point to values. They describe attitudes towards oneself, other people, society, and existence.

Person and *personality* imply something about a confrontational human being who faces the surrounding world as original and independent, a human being who is free and alive. To be a person and a personality is to express a specific temperament, a particular mind or psyche, a character who can be perceived and experienced by others. "Person" or "personality" signifies something substantial, something visible that makes lasting impressions and marks.

The person stands apart and is therefore a natural *authority*. The person is different from others by his/her nature, distinctive psychological qualities, moral opinions, or shortly by spirit. The person *is* a moral human being internally, not from any outer rules or norms, but just as a matter of course. In many situations, the person becomes a reminder of what is real and decent.

This understanding of the person can explain why the personal can be construed as alarming.

The person has a freedom that others may easily envy. Because the fear of freedom runs deep in people who live in the modern welfare state, the person and the personal can provoke anxiety. Additionally, because the person first and foremost is a human being who cares, who gets involved, and has ambition, he or she will often seem bothersome and uncomfortable to be around. Any culture that is based on the interests of the collective and the sameness of individuals, will view the person as a threat to the status quo.

The creative power of the person can also be regarded as offensive. A creative person will not be controlled by accepted practices nor be in complete control at all times. This is why the personal creates fear in others and also in oneself; the creative force intrudes and can transform life.

Building a life and a view of humanity based on the content of this concept of the person, personal, and personality will result in the creative and engaged human being. This human being can relate to his or her surroundings and relationships in a variety of ways, depending on how open the world is, the degree of acceptance and communication.

The person is first and foremost one who *meets*, faces others and reality in the eyes. This is not someone who is isolated from fellowship. On the contrary, the person has empathy for others, worries about them and their development. He/she may need to take distance to confront and try to change, reform, and revolutionize. The person is still an inescapable part of the fellowship and draws sustenance from relating to it and participating in it. The concept of person makes it possible to realize true fellowship and intersubjective reality.

In philosophical thought, these concepts have religious and metaphysical connotations, indicating spiritual values and relationships with groups of people who accept ties of friendship and solidarity.

This view of humanity becomes positive, the human being itself has an innate value and the goal of existence is to further and protect spiritual values. This means that the person is faithful, a "believer." He/she believes both in what it means to be a person and in the values of the personal.

In my philosophical context, person, personality and personal will be used to emphasize human beings as spirit, as a "I" or a "Self," and at the same time the person as filled with free will, morals and value. The person is not the opposite of fellowship but to emptiness, lack of engagement, lack of meaning, to the stereotype, the role-dominated and the mechanical human being. The contrast is difficult to concretize because it is about values, especially values that represent the a-personal and the materialistic human being.

Personalism oppose any view of humanity that reduces it to some kind of exemplar, a copy of everybody else or a social role, it is about quality and value, and for the opposite of reductionism and cynicism.

B. An *individual* can best be understood as a quantitative determination. The individual is an exemplar of the human species. The term *individual* indicate a wish to distinguish the one from the masses. To be an individual means to be counted as one, instead of one of many. "Individual" says nothing about one's inner qualities. The individual is different from others as one drop of water is different from other drops.

This is also the case if the subject is the individual's behavior. When a human being is seen as an individual it is dissociated from the masses, and others. This type of human being is special or eccentric simply because they stay outside. All individuals have this same characteristic: they stay out on the crowds. In this quantitative sense, there is no difference between outsiders. Any exceptionality that the individual may have, any unique character, is a result of withdrawal, not of any inner strength or any substance.

The determination of the quality of the individual can explain how the terms individual and individuality can easily contain particular political overtones in a social democratic society. They are often linked to reactionary political ideologies. Here, the "individual" is synonymous with someone who does not consider the collective or the weak. The "individual" is viewed as an egotist, egocentric, or worst of all, an elitist.

This is a reasonable interpretation since the individual comes with separation. The better the individual excludes others, the more noticeable he or she becomes as an individual. Exclusion or diminishment of the group and others highlights the individual only.

The one who consider him/herself as individual in this sense will always need to break out of the group and become a perpetual deserter and interrupter. The individual can easily become self-worshipper, one who must continually and at any price emphasize his or her differences from others. The will of the individual is precisely to be different.

In some contexts, this could of course be viewed as something positive. Because of the constant need to break out, the individual initiates changes, becomes a mover. By breaking out of set patterns of behavior, by refusing to live a conventional life, the individual can periodically drive progress, be a leader. Individuals become therefore good rebels, but the rebellions they start are often chaotic and full of contradictions. The individual's goal is never to join the masses, or to let the masses join him or her, and it is definitely not to create a synthesis, to make a better life for everybody a reality.

This concept of the individual provides a foundation for a view of humanity and society. Individuals present themselves as unavoidably lonely. There is a barrier between the individual and the society, "the others." As a result, the individual can easily feel like a stranger in the world, lonely, empty and meaningless. The ability to truly join a fellowship has not been developed.

Interestingly, in this philosophical context, the concepts of the individual and the masses become contrary but not contradictory opposites. They do not exclude each other. Each of them presupposes the other and needs the other to exist. Each adds content to the other. Should the concept of the individual disappear, so does the concept of the masses. Each is part of the same category of thought, part of the same quantitative mathematical content. There is no principal difference with regard to quality and inner characteristics when the human being is understood as an individual or as a member of the masses.

To the extent that a human being becomes a member of the masses, or the crowd, or an ingredient in a series of components, or an individual, ethically it means the same thing and could be due to a completely random set of facts. If the individual's need to rebel disappears, he or she will easily re-join the group without making any changes. This is probably what happens to youthful rebels when they begin to take on responsibilities and want a career. Radical positions are often simply an expression of a deep need to *seem* different and to be viewed as *somebody*.

C. The term *human being* is also a quantitative description. The purpose of the word is to distinguish humanity from all other living creatures on earth and in heaven. The word demonstrates the fact that human beings are earthly creatures, who both belong to and rule the earth. Because all the other species that human beings are different form, the concept tend to have some diffuse qualitative determination but without conclusive consequences for human relations.

Human means likewise that which is neither divine nor animal. The word refers to typical characteristic of which separate human beings from other species that they are naturally compared with. Especially one considers reason and language in these differences, the attributes that human beings want to think that only they have. Additional noble attributes also come to mind such as mercy, empathy, self-sacrifice, and humility, attributes that one thinks animals are incapable of. Only men/woman is humane.

This means that if human beings rank high above animals, they still are below God. Human beings make mistakes, are weak, pitiful, and wretched when viewed with divine eyes. They have many characteristics, feelings, and habits that (the Christian) God cannot have.

In a philosophical context, the concepts are tendentious and biased. Human beings are elevated above all other life forms, making them something magnificent in their own eyes, while animals become symbols for lesser life forms. The concepts are anthropological and can be damaging to our attitudes towards other earthly beings.

But the concepts also have a positive connotation in that human beings are charged with caring for themselves as well as all other life forms and the earth. They give human beings a sense of responsibility and challenge them to impose humane, as opposed to "bestial," brutal and gruesome, values and norms.

Simultaneously, *human being* and *human* become reminders of innate human insignificance and contain a challenge to people so that none will believe that they are 'somebody'. In truth, it is God who is strong, all-powerful, and just. These words can exalt and degrade depending on the perspective.

These concepts also have connotations in a political or cultural context. They refer to democratic and humanistic values, both to Christian and atheist or humanist ethics. These concepts become therefore often empty and conventional, lacking clarity. *Human* and *humanity* are mainly a formal classification, a reminder that one is neither animal nor God, and of consequence only to particular groups and individuals.

As a platform for a view of humanity, these concepts are therefore fairly innocuous. They offer no concrete, ethical, or practical norms and can develop feelings of either arrogance or inferiority in the users.

D. *Mass man* is a limitation of the term human being and offers a more distinct contrast to both *the person and the individual*. The Spanish philosopher *Jose Ortega y Gasset* analyzes this concept in *Massenes oprør* (Oslo, Gyldendal norsk forlag, 1934). Let me refer the characteristics of the concepts below.

The masses, says Ortega, can be anybody. "The mass is all who without particular grounds add to oneself a special importance—for good or evil—but which regards oneself as average, and nevertheless does not shiver, but is pleased when he notices that he is as everybody else."[3]

This modern human type implies a leveling out in all respects. Mediocrity becomes the main ideal, and the central values are comfort, self-righteousness, aimlessness, and self-indulgence. Mass man is characterized by the spoiled child's psychology. It acknowledges nothing outside of itself. All measures for good and evil, beauty and ugliness are taken from his or her own spontaneous and capricious tastes. Mass man is him/herself everything, without responsibility, serving only in the most trivial way. It has a hardened, isolated soul, says Ortega, and is intellectually petrified. Therefore it does not care to offer reasons for its opinions, but focuses instead on forcing its views on others.

Derision is the key tone for the mass man. It takes nothing seriously and acts as if any action can be recalled and means nothing. In actuality, mass man lacks morals and refuses to be placed under any authority and is thereby free from any conscious need to serve and to have responsibilities.

Something interesting happens to human beings, writes Ortega, when they become mass man/woman. "In this way, what was mere quantity, multitude, is converted into quality: namely the common quality, the social man as undifferentiated from other men, but repeating an ordinary type. What have we gained by this conversion of quantity into quality?"[4]

In my opinion, what one has gained is precisely irresponsibility, self-righteousness, and self-aggrandizement. Just as the young lord or lady from the days of the nobility, could feel like someone without having achieved anything, so mass man/woman gains status in its own eyes. He/she awards itself with honors simply because it exists and believes it alone deserves it.

The political connotations of this concept are well known. All liberation movements that don't demand anything of their supporters and are not concerned with new duties, but merely concentrate on new rights, often means the liberation of mass. The same is true of movements that do not treat their opponents as persons and do not credit them any rights or dignity. The mass man/woman is worshipped by all movements that hate the thought of the person.

The values evoked by this concept are either conventional or primitive, depending on whether time will allow for a possibility to gain new social goods. In primitive periods there are random but strong feelings that define action and choice. Mass man must be led and gladly rides the wave of the day, as long as he or she does not have to produce anything. Mass man seeks the movement for the movement's sake but does not dare move outside the group and never offers views that are different from the group. It is opportunistic and is along for the ride when there are short-term benefits to be had.

These three main concepts—person, individual and human being—can be used in daily speech interchangeably. But in my use, they will be used according to the philosophical analysis that has been offered here.

Anyone who wants to express something reasonable and central about human life and its qualities, or the possibility for quality, is sooner or later forced to begin with the concepts of person, personality, and the personal. Only these concepts can be used to distinguish between human beings and draw boundaries in the human realm. It is not true that we are all persons or that we are always personal. Rather, it is true that we are all persons now and then, and we can in fact all express ourselves as persons more and more often.

Simultaneously, it is important to note that at any given time, we can all live in all of these different dimensions and that there are connections between them. We are all objects, stereotypes, limited, and dominated by the roles we play, and continually choosing the lifestyle of individuals or mass man. It is also necessary for all of us to relate to the rest of the world and the possibility that there is a God and a devil.

But we can't escape moral or creative demands, nor completely avoid viewing others and ourselves as persons. These dimensions enable us to become multidimensional beings while the tension this creates defines our goals and the paths we have to take in life. We are constantly forced to find ourselves in relation to these different possibilities. No one can avoid the challenge that exists in locating the bridge between the individual and the collective. When you answer this challenge, you will inevitably experience the personal; the person is the bridge.

Chapter II

Towards the Person

AN OLD NOMENCLATURE DOES not necessarily reflect the way things are today. Language use can be shaped by ancient habit or by conventions and wishful thinking. Therefore clarifying the use of language is just the beginning. It is also important to clarify reality and make probably that the words have references. Finally, it is necessary to describe and lay down boundaries within this reality.

As *Emmanuel Mounier* says, we don't become persons by naivité.[5] Expressing yourself as a person is an undertaking, a job, often difficult and demanding. But from what I can tell, it may be the only necessary work that all human beings have in common, despite the conditions of their time.

We could also compare this process to birth. Becoming a person is to strive to be reborn as a living spirit, a soul, a complete being; there are many words that could be used. To me this birth seems to be a natural, necessary process. In the human being there is a deep longing for freedom, meaning, truth, goodness, and beauty, which must be expressed. The person becomes a reality that keeps growing on.

The innate becomes visible when one choose side, choose to see the positive possibilities that are always present, instead of the negative, just like the proverbial glass that can truthfully be described as either half-full or half-empty. Where people are concerned, the negative and positive scenarios are often both *true*. But the critical point is whether one's attention is focused on the former or the latter.

What you focus on will determine both actions and choices. If the individual and mass man/woman is the half-empty people, nobody, then the person is the half-full or completely filled human being. To develop towards the person, is much about the ability to see and experience innate, positive possibilities.

Three Stages of Human Being

Personal development can be understood as growth of an ethical nature, as three distinctly different phases that each human being must pass through in the relationship with oneself and others. When the person is liberated and matured, these phases will also appear as choices. It is possible to integrate the dimensions of mass man and the individual in the personal. One also sees that each phase in this process has its own unique advantages and disadvantages, its own price, reward, and punishment.

The human ethical development can be seen as a road from the mass man, via the individual to the person.

During childhood and adolescence, everyone goes through the phase of the mass man/woman.

All of us begin as part of the masses. We are literally mass man, completely absorbed by others, or more accurately, by one other human being. As a fetus in the womb, we are nourished by the female and return our excretions back into her body. This existence is an intimate cycle, where two people are symbiotically bound to one another for nine months.

Our earliest years are only a little less symbiotic. The physical dependence is so great, that without our parents' care, we would die. Mentally, we are intertwined with our parents for many years, especially the one with whom we spend the most time. Should he or she leave us, we cry, and we rejoice when he or she returns. That same symbiotic feeling, that deep dependence, can seize the adult. It has been shown that some mothers are unable to distinguish between the needs of her children and her own.[6] Some men who have committed incestuous acts have explained that they were convinced that the child wanted the sexual contact with them and enjoyed it.

For many parents and children, emotional symbiosis can become so great that they never really leave each other and are unable to live an independent life. Parents live and breathe for their children (a very descriptive expression) and children become dependent upon their parents' approval, affirmation, and adoration throughout their lives.

For most this close relationship during infancy and childhood is often so intense that it is very natural to describe the relationship between parents (especially mother) and children as a many-armed body, as *Elias Canetti* does in *Crowd and Power (Masse und Macht, 1960)*. The child, he says, becomes the mother's extra stomach: "A mother is one who gives her own body to be eaten."[7] And "Her passion is to give food. . . Her behavior appears selfless and is so if one regards her as a separate unit, as one single human being. But what has really happened is that she now has two stomachs instead of one, and keeps control of both.[8]"

Similarly, the mass man/woman and especially their political leaders can in the same way easily be experienced as a body with multiple limbs. As a people with one goal, synchronized in action and language, the masses act as somnambulistic automatons. Each human being becomes a marionette, governed by leaders who in turn are governed by the needs and wants of the masses. Both good and charitable deeds can be launched from the common body. The leaders are the head of the masses; the masses are the stomach and limbs for the leaders. They reflect each other, like a mother and her newborn child. In the 20th century, there have been numerous examples of mass movements with many different ideological foundations. The single mob is also an expression of such symbiosis, the admiration of commanders and leaders is a sign that a mob is about to be formed.

But this stage is not only expressed in political movements, mobs or gangs. It is also normal, conventional life situations in which anything that needs to be done, can be done by everyone, with no special preparation or engagement. As when fixing an outcome for a sports competition and deciding on a winning time after everyone has reached the goal; or quiz shows and family games. When the environment is dominated by values of similarity, and everyone wants to be alike and do what everyone else does. The mass-stage is often characterized by the need for satisfaction of the desire of likeness through easily attained means, like getting attention by following fashion with clothes and appearance.

This stage can also include simply cultivating one's own family and disappearing into the nuclear family, forming the foundations for new generations. Here too one attains honor of sorts without doing anything special, just by having children and living like everyone else. It is acceptable to brag freely about and praise one's children and grandchildren, and therefore oneself, without this being conspicuous. One becomes someone simply by emulating those one thinks are special, in this case, one's own relatives. This return to the home, prioritizing family and free time, can also fulfill a need to feel like somebody important through others, with no need to perform any achievement of note.

This cultivation of home and the nuclear family may explain the growth of mass man in modern society. In the absence of class divisions and nobility, and through the development of a society in which most are able to participate, the nuclear family's values have greater force than in other societal types. These values put private quantitative consumption in center, to create equality inside the group, between man and woman, adult and child. Ideally, men and women shall have the same roles and do the same work; as soon as the child's age permits, adult and child should become friends. Simultaneously, the ideal suggests that the family should present a united front to the outside world. (This façade does not prevent that many families may have reached solid relationships based on the person.)

Increasingly people seek to become like everyone else and to belong to groups. In Norway, there are countless clubs, societies, organizations, and institutions that have no concrete purpose. It is as though people can't get together without a membership. One participates as any member instead of someone who desires personal interaction with others. This wish to belong to a group can hide the need to have the same opinions as everyone else who count as "somebody" and with whom one agrees. It is in the company of these others that the process of likeness can start; you have to meet to know what to mean. The most typically mass man in this context will always try to represent the majority.

Mass man may thus be more or less concrete and cerebral. Masses based on opinions of the masses are probably something typical for the 21st century. As I have written elsewhere: "When people do not have their fellowship in the outer world, in the necessity that arise from primary industry, relatives or colleagues at work, the opinions will replace this necessity. In their need for wholeness, the opinions of the crowd become a substitute for essential fellowship of life.

Mass opinions begin and end with meanings. The meanings become the treasures or relics of the "tribe." Nuances of opinions and renegades threaten the group, there is a limit for how complex, small, or powerless a mass opinion can allow itself to be and still exit."[9]

The phenomenon of mass opinion can somewhat explain the many intrigues, battles and peelings off that we so often find in the life of social organizations, and perhaps especially in political parties.

This does not prevent certain groups from sharing some opinions through personal processes. But, as I will address later, persons often disagree and do not fear having differences of opinion, they assume of course, that no one agrees about "everything."

Characteristically, mass man will seek honors and status by being just like everyone else. This is not as paradoxical as it sounds, since there will always be someone who cannot or will not participate in the fight to become like everyone else—even in the modern welfare state. A culture will never become so homogenous that everyone can be exactly alike, nor will all groups become one great mass. Nature ensures that there are deep differences between human beings, so does the individuals.

Sooner or later, for however long a period of time, every human being will want to move on to the next phase. This phase I will term the *individualistic* phase. As previously mentioned, in this phase it becomes very important to differentiate yourself, at any price, from the "others." And noteworthy, these "others" are the same "others" that mass man wants to imitate.

Opposition becomes centrally, it is often expressed symbolically at a very early age through defiance and temper tantrums. Just as the little child often is expressing mass man, the teenager expresses the individual. To be a teenager means precisely to be free from the parent-body, the nuclear family, and breaks apart the unit that has been expressed outwardly, and often inwardly, through norms such as loyalty and solidarity. This happens despite the fact that the teen often joins a gang and is a mass man/woman in that connection. As relates to the parents, the teen is the individual itself.

The *individual* wants accurately not to be used by parents, not to be their extra stomach, head, legs or arms, treasure or heir. The individual wants only to be one's own. This can often mean that it does not want to resemble the rest of the family, not believe the same things, not dress like them, nor eat and live like them. The main goal of the teenager is to separate physically and psychologically from the old group, the family, so that he or she are clearly visible and explicit different. Parents appear hopeless, part of a distant past, which mean that they are the group that can remove the valuable individuality from the teen. And that is actuality many parents try to raise their children to become as they themselves are. The result may be that the family, suddenly get an artist or some other deviant individual in their periphery.

The artist is a typical individualist. To him or her, the artist, "the others" are everyone, the establishment, bourgeois society. The artists often want to break with all traditions, both in time and space, to him or her, everything begins anew. Nothing from the others should survive through them. Such people may also seek out their gangs, like bohemian environments, to gain inspiration for the final showdown with the threat against originality or genius. The intense controversies are often a cover for the fear of being infected with normalcy, and becoming a mass man/woman again.

If the artist can be considered a "true" individualist, the most common type is the quarreler. He and she who always disagree, always need to add a comment, and minimize what others have said, is the individual who seek to deviate for the sake of deviation and for self-promotion. It is quite possible that in our own society the easiest way to promote your individuality is through quarreling and deviant opinions; the meanings masses are so absolutely the most dominant.

The individualist phase is also one that all people pass through, more or less thoroughly. But for many, youthful rebellion can be temporary, and they return to the masses. This time not, as weak children or teens without their own economy and status, but as powerful parents. They renew the old symbiosis and become its leader. Similarly, a previously radical rebel or a pioneering artist may become a frequently used member of committees, councils, and boards. He/she have secured their power and can therefore rejoin the "others," and desire dialogue and cooperation. Therefore many individuals, are fakers, their rebellion is based on the need to have power sooner than they should, before their natural time has arrived. Because individualism is a quantitative concept that consists of a mathematical deviation, individualists are in reality representatives for parental and societal power.

This also reveals the connection between the mass man or woman and the individual; individuals come into existence because they, as the mass man/woman, want to have recognition for something they actually have never achieved nor deserve recognition for. The difference is that this longing for honors takes opposite paths. Mass man seeks the ordinary, while the individual seeks the extraordinary.

The third phase one may choose to enter is becoming a *person*. Maturity has been reached during the stage of conflict between the individual and mass man/woman. Then one is independent, conscience about oneself, convinced of one's uniqueness, and takes this for granted without the need to talk about it all the time. One can give of self and receive tenfold back. The more generous and honest one becomes, the more successful one become as a person.

With this stage comes *the living fellowship*. The collective is not any more a mass, but fellowships of friends acting and thinking independently as persons. This fellowship is not synchronized but maintained through open and honest communication.—Since the person and the intersubjective are the main theme of this book, I will be brief at this point on this subject.

Each of the three phases has its advantages.

The life as mass man/woman may fill life with nostalgia and give promises of safety. As long as one is part of the large body, it may seem that one will always get what one need, and at the same time, be protected by others. There is safety in the masses, in the family, in the home, with those who are alike.

Canetti explains this with the fact that existence inside the masses temporarily removes guilt from people, allowing them to forget commands that hurt and wound.[10] Within the masses the human being is guilt-free because physically, he/she is part of all the others. Who gives the hand, toes, or head alone the blame for what the human being has done? During times of trouble, one must show solidarity and be unselfish. One simply has to, if the larger body is to continue as one. If all sacrifice themselves for the larger body, it can seem as if everyone will get everything they need from others.

The *individual* may make one yearns for heroism and feed everyone's dreams to become immortal and famous. Standing alone, against the many, for yourself, can seem as signs of nobility and give you pride and strength. As common wisdom would have it, this implies that one has become someone, and can, if the individual is lucky, gain a place in history. Despite their stage of development and ambitions, all individuals desire the mark of immortality. To get into as many history books as possible is the goal of the individual.

The *person* tempts because this stage offers hope and optimism. Through the person goes the road to a society of friends, sweethearts, partners, and a society based on dignity and trust. The fellowship in which you are seen as you truly are, is greatly to be preferred to the phase of the masses that is based on roles and stereotypical expectations, and to the individualistic stage in which one is either made a loser or given one of the exposed positions at the top.

Each stage has its own particular disadvantages.

The mass can easily turn on its own. Arms, legs, and eyes that no longer please, may be cut off. And leaders need to assert themselves as individuals will continually entail battles between leaders, which unavoidably affect the mass in the long run. When there is a shortage, the mass will split into smaller masses, into those that will receive and those who will not, into those who are equal and those who are more equal, as *George Orwell* describes in *Animal Farm*. (1948) Nostalgia can easily be succeeded by horror, as it is only when there is harmony within and the enemies clearly outside that the mass can offer safety to all of its members. When this stage is over, all individuals in principle are equally superfluous, since no one means more to anyone than any other. Therefore, the masses are free at any time, whenever necessary, to get rid of troublemakers, deviants, individuals, or the autonomous persons.

Additionally, an excess of members can create problems. When there are too many, they become replaceable; the mass and their leaders can easily and painlessly change limbs, and still survive.

Similarly, the *individual* can easily get into difficulties. Being an individual at any price is lonely. It can result in a destructive battle against others or oneself. The fruitful battle to reach personhood, do not necessarily become a success. The individual can be broken in the belief on its own majesty and end up not on a pedestal, but in a mass grave.

In the conflict between mass man and the individual, one may see the source of the inferiority complexes and megalomania. Mass man/woman, may feel themselves, not only as not anybody, but as nobody at all. It is only the others who *are*, they are everything. The individual can feel just opposite, the others are nothing, nulls, while itself is everything. Therefore the battle between mass man and the individual often becomes total; the question becomes who has the right to exist, there is not enough existence for everyone.

Neither *the person* is guaranteed success. Friendship and community, like all other deeply human communication, are dependent upon others. If others do not want to talk, do not want to be open and receive, the person can be even lonelier than the individual. The individual has no need to communicate, only to be worshipped. The person can easily be broken on the longing for fellowship, for dialogue, doing something together, *communicare*, if there is no one with whom to communicate. Growing in order to live in love and friendship presupposes that others think one is loveable and that those others are praiseworthy to one-self, that both parties really are able to give both friendship and love. Communication that is filled with love is not simple or an easy way to live.

Parallel with these phases of human development are certain fundamental ethical positions.

Mass man/woman is a hedonist. The primary goal is pleasure: Good is defined as anything that gives the most pleasure to one-self and one's fellows. The good serves one's own group and the goal is to satisfy any and all needs that the mass may have at any given time. When the conditions are reversed, and the mass do not gets its needs satisfied, blood lust and revenge becomes the norm. Good is then defined as anything that reestablishes the group's honor and satisfies the group's needs. Harmless self-indulgence quickly turns into bloody revenge depending on how external changes influence the solitary and the group situation.[11] Mass man has no feelings for or understanding of people who belong to other groups or masses. Because they have membership elsewhere, they are rather a potential enemy than a friend.

The *individual* is a hedonist too but characterized probably more by cynicism and indifference. To the individual, good is anything that serves his or her struggle to stand out against the background of the others, and that helps it to get attention on the expense of all others. Cynicism, can become utilitarianism, anything that is useful to promote the individual becomes a moral good.

Simultaneously the individual can easily become a persecutor. Part of the fight for visibility is the fight against others who might hide the individual, threaten its celebrity, or step on its toes. As previously stated, mass man and the individual have a great deal in common, not least in the moral dimension. They both lack of over-arching value, no one and nothing are above them and theirs. They themselves are the goal and the means to their ends are sacred through them.

In contrast, the *person* does have overarching values, or ideals, which are not attached to social status, economic or practical goals. These goals are eternal and form the person's beliefs. The ethics can be called Christian or Humanist, depending on one's definition, but not depending on one's experiences. Only the person is able to act for the community's best since the person alone acts from values that promote true fellowship. The person's qualitative advantages are therefore not based in any biological or psychological qualities but first and foremost on the moral qualities that the person is willing to realize, strive to do, and to set as an ideal.

Finally, let me emphasize that these three phases or types can occur simultaneously, in one and same human being. That depends on one's relationship to oneself and the different groups to which one naturally belong. But the phases can of course coincide with age and experience. Most commonly, it is probable that people move among the three phases according to a given situation and a choice.

Characteristics of the Person

Portraying oneself fulltime, as an individual, a mass man/woman, or a person is in the long run an expression of a choice. If people act unconsciously in their lives or in their relationships, they will switch back and forth amongst the three types periodically, experiencing all of the advantages and disadvantages. Being a person is not necessarily more or less difficult than being an individual or one of the masses, but it is highly probable that if one consciously choose to be a person, it will result in a life that is more truthful, more genuine, and more valuable.

In this section, I want to offer a more general, philosophical description of the person and the person's fundamental characteristics. As a model, we must imagine an ideal human being who consistently managed to carry out and to live according to personal values in his or her own life. Jesus Christ was such a person.

First let me describe how the person can be experienced. The Scottish philosopher and Quaker *John Macmurray* wrote the following: "When I meet the kind of person who is exceptionally real for me, I recognize him because there is no getting over the fact that he is there. He can't be overlooked, even when he says nothing and does nothing. He is emphatically *there*. More than that, he is all there — not in the ordinary sense, but literally. There is a wholeness and completeness about him that I sense in some strange way. And then, he is very much himself... There is always a curious simplicity and definiteness about him — a quietness which is sure of itself. Not the quietness of what is dead, but the quietness of a steady flame... A very real person seems to have a flame in him as it were that shines through and makes him transparent. He isn't necessarily brilliant intellectually or emotionally powerful. He may or may not be; but if he is clever, you hardly notice it, it is so simple; indeed you notice *him* so much more than his qualities. He is significant, and significant just by being himself, not through any particular qualities or peculiarities that he possesses. And he is significant because he is vital. Yet the vitality is not necessarily a fullness of physical activity, or even physical strength because it shows equally well, perhaps even better, in repose. It is rather a fullness of life, a completeness of life, and an inherent livingness about him."[12]

I can expand on that description by sketching 10 fundamental qualities you will find in *persons*, regardless of their age, status, gender, or situation.

A. The person's foremost characteristic is *engagement*. The person is a participant, a player, already inside a fellowship. The person needs no encouragement to become engaged, or to sit and wait for offers, to be asked. In a society of persons, everybody will be at the dance floor at one's own initiative. As Mounier says: "People always speak of 'engagement' as if it depended upon ourselves: but *we are engaged*, embarked, already involved. Abstention is only a delusion."[13]

But engagement must not be confused with continual interference in other people's business. Not least of all, this engagement is thinking, understanding. The person is awake, conscious, sees patterns and structures, understands group dynamics, and is aware of his or her own role in the group. He/she is attentive, not by will or analytical, because mentally, they can "dance," as part of the group.

B. The person has a consistent *moral positions and outlooks* on the whole of existence. He/she *experience* all that happens within the frame of good and evil, experience values, and are aware of ethical results and consequences of actions. This ethical experience ensures that all engagement is directed towards justice and is engaged in a battle against all that may trivialize and reduce, all that denies the innate possibilities and abilities of human beings to overcome the common and habitual.

This moral character must be limited as it relates to the moralistic. I view moralism as morals used towards others, without bringing oneself into the situation. The moralist lacks moral intuition and has no feeling for the ethical reality. He/she get their morals from conventions, norms, or rules, and not from experienced and tested life. That is why the morals of the moralists (?) often seem empty and hypocritical, and moralists themselves can be ethically blind and insensitive.

The morals of the person have its origin from inner experiences. He/she has learned through pain and suffering, joy and beauty, what is good and what is evil. The person does not follow conventional morals and can easily go against accepted norms.

C. The engagement and morals of the person is guided by universal *spiritual values*. These values include truth, goodness, beauty, love, and friendship. In this way the human beings get a place in relation to something independent of and greater than self and private life. That "something" is always of a metaphysical, universal, and spiritual nature, and is independent of material, economic, or private relationships. Materialistic values are subordinate to the spiritual. Spiritual values define a person's goals, while all other types of values serve as means towards that goal.

D. The person is free. *Freedom* is a quality that comes from within the personal. Freedom consists first and foremost in the person being him/herself, letting that self be, not letting other people or impersonal conventions take control. The person expresses and develops on their own conditions and within their own possibilities, and are, in a matter of speaking, the flower of their own seed.

Freedom also belongs to a person's dignity, natural pride, and feeling of honor. Persons assert their human worth and will not be commanded nor wish to command others. Neither internal condition nor external orders can determine the actions and choices of persons. Persons accept the freedom to choose for themselves and accept the consequences.

This freedom implies everything we understand about human rights, legal rights, and justice associated with (alleged) crimes. The person demands to be viewed and treated as free by others, including the state and society.

To assert the freedom of the person is thus both to underline the nature of humanity and the social, legal, and political consequences that result because of this.

E. The person meets the world with *friendship*, *love*, and *sympathy*. The person is trustful and affectionate, able to see the positive innate possibilities in all human beings. Respect for community and all people is the foundation for this attitude towards others. Through these feelings, the person becomes observant; love adds a sixth sense, a third eye, while hate and repulsion only blind. It follows from this that the person expects to meet friendliness and is open and accepting.

F. The person can also *confront* their surroundings forcefully. Genuine love implies honesty, the will to correct missteps, and redirect if necessary. There will always be confrontation if shortsighted, materialistic, and impersonal values and actions take priority.

The person keep track not only of how he/she and others are but also of how they all are becoming.

G. Furthermore, the person is *complete*. Notwithstanding their engagement in metaphysical and spiritual values, persons are citizens of two worlds. Persons are *both body and soul*. Commitment leads the person into the here and now. Mounier says: "By its refusal to leave me wholly transparent to myself, the body takes me constantly out of myself into the struggles of mankind. By solicitation of the senses it pushes me out into space, by growing old it acquaints me with duration, and by its death, it confronts me with eternity. We bear the weight of its bondage..."[14]

The body fulfills the soul.

H. The next important characteristic is, as already mentioned by Macmurray, the person's *presence*. The person is always present, always part of the situation, with the others, in relationships, and at the same time entirely in his or her own skin. He or she is not passing through, not on the way to another meeting, a date with someone else, or living in a dream world, a lost past, or a yet to be realized future. That immediate presence explains why the person is experienced as a whole, something substantial, and why the person experiences him or herself that way.

I. The person has the ability to *decentralize*. The person is just as much present with others as with him/herself, a living complements, always a companion. He/she doesn't hold tight in anxiety or indifference to self or shut away the inner life so that others do not catch a glimpse of who he/she is. The person let others gain insight into that self when it is natural and necessary to do so, but never indiscriminately. The person expresses many nuances and exhibit complexity. There is no inner hierarchy even internally, no need to place reason on top and emotions on the bottom. The person carefully distributes power within, amongst his/her many sides, possibilities, and characteristics. The person projects inner democracy and create democracy him/herself.

J. The person at the core is *communication*. The person can reach out without any strain, turn towards others, listen, receive and give. The person is always willing to gamble, always willing to see whether there is a possibility to meet. This is an expression for a natural tendency, an agreeable perception, and not a reason induced decision that dictates a need to communicate. Communication is an important value in and of itself.

Experiencing a person is to experience a psychophysical whole, a personality, and moral character. Developing into a person or maintaining oneself as person means that one is also developing wholeness, psychosocial harmony, and morals. It is not possible to tell what comes first or possible to choose what may be more important than the other. The person has many facets.

The Hero

There are few possibilities to the person in an impersonal or indifferent society such as ours. Clearly, the masses and individuals have free reign. This is especially apparent in the visions that society has of our heroes and the heroic and the roles they play.

A hero is normally viewed as a winner, prevailing against all odds. The hero get the job done; the lonesome cowboy reinstates law and order, the great general makes all the critical decisions, the daring adventurer has to trust himself when facing all dangers. The hero is the outsider, the lucky boy who wins the princess and the entire kingdom.

But the ordinary view of the hero is inconsistent with the countless ways individuals try to become heroes in the modern welfare state. The hero is not always alone, but often with a group, not the obvious winner, but just as likely the loser. The hero does not have to be the good one. He or she can be a villain just as likely. In the chaos of existence, the role of hero is possible for many, but not everyone strives for the same type of heroic deed.

The need to become a hero may also, according to *Ernest Becker*, be satisfied by different heroic systems that the individual creates for himself.[15] These systems can be anything from a successful conventional life with a career and family to neuroses and criminal activity. Modern individuals define their heroism quite obstinately and often the exact opposite of what is normally expected.

According to social democratic thought, the losers often get the glory of the hero. Viewed as heroes treated unfairly, they were up against such difficult tests that they were doomed to failure. This is especially the opinion when the hero is from an oppressed group.

In other words, our society has systems for heroes adapted to the masses and to individuals. This is revealed in the confusion about the content of the hero's role. The mass-man or woman, as mentioned, award themselves honors for nothing, while the only purpose of the individual is to call attention to oneself compared to all others.

The traditional view of the hero is consistent with the person. The person is a hero due to self-confidence, the courage to stand alone, make his and her own decisions, and assert a uniquely communicative mind in life.

The person lives outside of the conventional definition of heroes and the judgment of others, and judge alone, by engagement and actions. There is a price to pay, in most contexts it will be an achievement and an accomplishment. Like in the fairy tales, one must discover that one has a goal, shall carry out a singular task, conscious of the fact that one becomes tested, be able to receive help from the modest and the wretched, that which no one else respects, always ready to get back up when knocked down. In the personal reality, there are countless challenges, and it is always possible to make mistakes and to lose. The list of tasks is endless.

When compared to the person the loser can be seen as someone without the will to meet challenges, unable to submit the self to be tested, unable to help and give to others. The loser is the human being that cannot be responsible or stands alone, but demands the right not to fight and still expects to win.

To become a hero, a person, will again and again create possible confrontations, reckonings, reconciliations, and growth. The hero must constantly fight to protect access to personal reality, hold on to the soul and express its reality.

Heroic deeds are expressed first and foremost in private life, even one's own body. They consist of letting one's own voice be heard, letting others gain insight into one's feelings and thoughts, and one dares to intrude when justice demands. In daily life, this means being responsible, for self, others and the relationship. Only he or she who wins their internal ethical battles is heroes.

In other words, the hero is the one who see that daily life is not uncomplicated, well-ordered, good, safe, and boring reality. But is able to see complexity, chaos, evil, and ambiguous, the ambiguity and tension that is present in every meeting and relate to it through engagement and action. Naturally, the hero is not always successful. The hero is therefore conscious of real possibility of defeat that lies ahead; the hero stands in the intersection between victory and defeat, in the effort to overcome passivity, laziness, and weak will.

The Person: Being together

The need for the hero can therefore be understood as press from the personal. It intrudes on dreams, hopes, and plans. Somewhere out there in the distance tempts the hero, that on closer scrutiny, will be seen as the human being as a person. It is this living wholeness that one seeks.

Thus the personal manifests itself not just as a threat, but also as an offer and a temptation. If one thinks that it is easy to become a person, one is likely left with the individualistic, one thinks that it is enough to appear as different. Only he or she that in honor and respect develop the personal, recognize the innate demands of the personal places will be able to find oneself as a person.

The personal may be a shock. When the human being is becoming a person, he or she will wake up. Both, oneself, others and the relationship emerge in a new way. Existence and the world around can easily seem empty, meaningless, and barren. Even one's own ego can seem foreign and worthless. Other people seem not only boring and inexpressive, not to take hold of, the person feels quite alone in the world. The Ego in personal growth finds itself surrounded by mass men/woman and individuals, it will experience a society that don't offers space, and conventional relations without meaning.

This view can stay destructive. When the ugliness of existence is unveiled, one can easily be blinded by what emerges. One does not necessarily see what created this new consciousness, but simply remain in the shock of what one believes one has learned. As a result, one can turn away from the surroundings in disgust, and despair, maybe choose a self-destructive lifestyle, and even suicide.

But the understanding does not come from what has been understood, is not identical with it. It comes from inside the person who is emerging. Emptiness and lack of meaning are something external. When the personal reveals how fragile interrelations are, the possibilities to do something are also revealed. The clues from the personal reveal the possibility for meaning and new life. There exist a next phase.

One can look at the personal as explanatory, and in the sense of the mind as enlightenment. Therefore, first and foremost, in the experience of the personal there is a challenge and an alarm, and awakens the experience of the personal. It must be understood as a supervisor.

People who suffer from emptiness and meaninglessness can see this as a sign of expression of the personal. It is important to accept this and allow the personal to haunt oneself. The destructive disappears as he/she try harder and more distinctly to express oneself as a person.

The personal becomes in the last run a chance for redemption. If one is able to endure emptiness and lack of meaning without running away, the personal will offer new meaning and new life. Existence grows richer, gains more depth, and bestows strong feelings of reality and closeness.

What happens first and foremost is that one stop expressing a role, ceases to be an 'it', and becomes an "I" or a "Thou."[16] Other people seem more complex, exciting, and distinctive. The relationships between oneself and others become far more flexible and richer in content than before.

Above all else, the person is first and foremost a company. The personal comes from something that is more than and greater than the individual emptied of meaning, and the stereotyped others, it points to another way of relation and living, gather the world together so that the person can go forth and fill it.

The person will be experienced as a companionship, both by others and him and herself. To use a misleading word, one can almost measure the development of a person by the degree of participation one experience or boredom. When one leaves another human being with the feeling of having experienced real communication and opinions, one has had a personal meeting. If one walks away with a feeling of emptiness and boredom, either oneself, the other one or both, did not managed to be present. Boredom is a lack of authenticity and dialog.

The fact that the person is a "being together" implies that anyone can learn to withstand loneliness and make it rewarding. Being alone with yourself is also being with someone, resting with someone and communicating with someone. One self is just as diverse as others. Only those who strongly censure their own feelings, thoughts, and spontaneous moods, frames of mind and whims will experience themselves as empty and boring. Within one's own inner reality, one can find a well of possibilities and partners for conversation.

Chapter III

Inner Reality

WHILE ENGAGING IN DISCUSSIONS about the conditions of the oppressed, especially women, I have realized that many do not have any real understanding of inner reality. The human being is viewed from the outside only, an empty sack that society must fill up. Our parents and community, through upbringing and social pressure, are supposed to deliver to us our possibilities, our actions, and even the content of our lives.

If the upbringing or environment is too destructive and too difficult, or lacking in some other way, conventional wisdom would have us believe that we are predestined to failure. This also applies to those who begin life under excellent conditions. Something peculiar and new, it is not supposed that the individual human being by him/herself is able to create.

These are the kinds of ideas that shape mass man and the individual. When people are convinced, that neither they nor others can fill their own selves, it becomes more difficult than it might otherwise be to experience both an inner and an interpersonal reality, including the wholeness of the person. Should this type of experience be rare, it is difficult to believe in and develop the personal.

We need a strong counter-culture, new ideas about human possibilities and prosperity, positive and optimistic ideas about ourselves. Ideas are also tools to shape ourselves, even if many safely may let things happen or let nature run its course. The growth towards the person is an inborn capacity.

The Experience of Existence

In our culture, it can be difficult to gain insight into our own inner reality. There are many obstacles to this experience, both external and internal.

Our external existence is a restless one. Noise, activity, deadlines and short-term so-called necessary duties, interfere with any insight. The inhibitions and taboos of individuals, limitations and convictions, lead also to blindness. If one is ashamed of oneself and one's inner thoughts, one avoids to look inside and do not wish to experience one's inner wholeness. The prejudices and stereotypes others may have about you will have the same effect. When others do not see one as a person or believe in one, it is sometimes easier to assume that one is wrong, than to insist that what one alone see and experience really does exist. Personal reality can easily turn into a question about who sees more clearly or who is most mature, less insane, or a question about power.

The question about one really is, is answered for everybody when they know in their entire body and soul that they really exist. This experience of existence is impossible to doubt, it is so strong that, it will shape the future and its quality.

In the history of philosophy, *Descartes*, among others, has found the starting point of his thoughts in this experience. He writes in *Discourse on Methods* "But then, immediately, as I strove to think of everything as false, I realized that, in the very act of thinking everything false, I was aware of myself as something real; and observing that truth: *I think, therefore I am*, was so firm and so assured that the most extravagant arguments the sceptics were incapable of shaking it, I concluded that I might have no scruple in taking it as that first principle for which I was looking."[17]

The first principle of philosophy for Descartes becomes the reality in the human beings own conscious experience. This means that inner reality is just as real as the external one, even if the content of the two realities also may be seen as completely different.

This inner reality is also a proof and source of the person. When a human being can grasp with its entire being that he/she exists, are *real*, the experience of existence has been set for the whole of the existence. This becomes a vision that allows renewal. The experience gives birth to the person. Should this experience later grow weaker, it will never entirely disappear, the impressions cannot be forgotten. Certain experiences take root in the mind forever.

The experience of one's own existence brings with it an assurance, a certainty that follows very few other experiences. It is like planting one's feet on firm ground after having been at sea for a lengthy period of time, as if entering a new dimension. It is also to expose fundamental structures and anatomies, see a reality where other rules apply than those that earlier had taken for granted. After this experience, one can return to normal life and see that it also contains more and something else than originally thought.

It is in this context that self-confidence and self-assurance are fully understood; the person may have reason to be confident, know him/her self and be certain of his or her own existence.

The Content of the Experience of Existence

First, let me try to describe this inner reality and emphasize that each of us is free to describe his or her own reality. But it is quite likely that the inner world has an approximately similar structure and form for all human beings.

A. The basic structure of inner reality comes forward as *movement*. In the internal, there is a flow, a modification, where the movement itself is central, not its extremes or contrasts. It is the pathway *from* the one *to* the other that is experienced.

With movement as the point of departure, the differences and the contradictory are largely dissolved. A dynamic picture of the personality is formed rather than a static one.

This is especially important regarding the experience of the relationship between our thoughts and feelings.

In our culture it is more or less acceptable that one shouldn't think while one feels, shouldn't be aware of feelings, and vice versa, thoughts should live in some disinterested vacuum.

This may be due to the belief that feelings are part of the real, natural, and instinctive human being, and therefore may be disturbed by thoughts. At the same time thoughts are seen as belonging to an intellectual superstructure.

This arises from the belief that feelings often are considered something with which people randomly fill themselves. Feelings are consumed, conjured up, and used as a narcotic. These kinds of feelings are quite easy to deflate. Should thoughts also be gathered in this way, from outside, from others, or are not reflections, they have no foundation. If the human being, do not think for him/herself, there is no connection between thoughts and emotions.

As a result, thoughts and feelings are often artificial. They are abandoned goods, impersonal phenomena that are neither felt nor thought, but rather presumed felt or thought. When the human beings let themselves be trained to feel what they are supposed to feel and to think correctly, there is no connection between their own thoughts and emotions. But it is also no connection between the people themselves and their thoughts and feelings.

Through the experience of existence, experiencing one's own moveable inner self, the personal, arise new wholeness between thought and emotion. Thoughts and feelings express an inner life, a reality. Both thoughts and feelings emerge out of the self or the ego, and are the property of the person, immediate responses to a direct acquaintance with reality.

Therefore, they will be diverse, nuanced, and fit together. A living human being cannot think without feeling and cannot feel without thinking. Thought registers all feelings and feelings walk hand in hand with the thought. A feeling that is not thought or a thought that is not felt becomes unreal, unseen, and unexperienced. They make no impression, nor internally on the human being or externally in communication with others.

Illuminated by inner wholeness of the personal, a thought will mirror a feeling and vice versa, so that you are able to feel your thoughts, feel whether they are good or evil, feel their vibrations and effects in a personal world. In the same experience, one can think emotions, think through their consequences for others and for oneself. Feelings give life and content to thoughts; thoughts give form and context to feelings. Division and chaos are transformed into a whole.

B. Inner reality has another fundamentally distinctive feature. It is always in the first person singular. The human beings cannot experience one's reality without saying: 'I'. I feel, I think, I learn and experience MYSELF. My own mobility cannot be experienced unless it is I who experiences it, unless I am completely involved in the experience both as the one who experiences and is experienced, both as subject and object. The sensation of the inner content is the self itself, that which is sensed and that which does the sensing are one and the same.

Usually, this may seem self-contradictory. But most of us may have experiences that tell us that it is possible, even something daily. When we touch, we can perceive the other's body and our own, experience from both the inside and outside. In those moments, the body can perform the perfect movement, and simultaneously feel and be self-aware. Our insight can illuminate the landscape of our thoughts. In the act of lovemaking, we are able to experience both ourselves and the other as one whole, even though, the border between the two as persons don't disappear. In the dialogue we can understand and acknowledge both the other and ourselves.

There is no constant and continuous barrier between the human being observing and experiencing and the inner world, when he or she is unified internally and able to say: *I am*. In this movement, the human being becomes whole, and experiences oneself as one. This first person singular experience constitutes or produces in that one particular moment a whole person who is able to say: I AM. Or I FEEL THE LIFE INSIDE ME! When that happens, the human being, become new to him or herself, becomes their own offspring, both the adult and the child.

C. A third characteristic of inner reality is precisely this *multiplicity*. Inside each one of us lives not only these so-called contradictions but also many voices and many rooms. We have possibilities that never disappear. We listen to our past, present, and future; the voices blend together into the choir of life. We become children, adults, and seniors simultaneously; we feel the child and the old person inside of us.

Not least of all, we feel how the gender stereotypes disappear. Our presumed female/feminine and male/masculine values vanish.[18] If outwardly we seem (or perhaps wish to seem) one-sided and role-dominated, inside we absolutely are not. Inside there is a complex collection of characteristics and traits. We are most definitely not either-or, but rather both-and. We are both man and woman—weak, passive, and self-effacing while at the same time strong, active and self-assertive. We are whole and can use that wholeness when we wish and must do so. It is life-threatening to believe that social roles have anything to do with inner personal reality.

In *Siddhartha, Hermann Hesse* puts it like this: "He no longer saw the face of his friend Siddhartha, instead he saw other faces, many, a long sequence, a flowing river of faces, hundreds of thousands, which all came and left, and yet all seemed to be there simultaneously, and all changed with Siddhartha."[19]

D. Time, also gets a new role in our lives, it is no longer composed of points on a line. It becomes rather a rhythm, a tempo that sometimes races along, sometimes just strolls along. Time can move in circles and return suddenly to something that has already happened. Remembering becomes returning or experiencing in a flash of the moment something that may happen years from now. Time is nothing outside of us, not a threat because it leads to death, but enrichment because it leads us on a journey into reality and inside ourselves.

Time becomes a process, determined by body and soul, of experiences, attitudes and values. The clock does not show time, we do. Such instruments are simply illustrative of natural cycles. Years pass, yet time can stand still, time can rush ahead, and all that an epoch contains can be over in a few minutes.

In this inner reality, time is a whole, fused with here and now.

E. A final characteristic is candor and amenability, the experience of being able to receive, of being filled with a self that seems far more than an ego or the usual consciousness one believes to be the entire self. This may also be experienced as being completely open and filled by something (body) outside of you. When you experience yourself, you can really open up to others or something else.

Self-preoccupation obstructs the experience of inner reality. Self-centered people are shut off from themselves. They are usually focused on how they want to seem to others.

Let me relate here one woman's description of being fully alive: "But one bright spring day—it was the 29th of May 1902 . . . so quiet, so invisible, this central occurrence in her life. Without sight or sound of speech or any human element she experienced in complete clarity knowledge of the great, releasing inner wonder. The "empty shell" broke. All weight and wind, the whole of the outer world sank. She could sense a living goodness, joy and light like a penetrating, clear, uplifting, all-encompassing and unambiguous reality deep inside. The first impression that popped into her head was...this is the great Mercy, this is God, and nothing else is as *real* as this."[20]

Identity and Personality

Identity is a concept of contradictions. It means both to identify someone in a singular way, for example by name, personal information, conformity and sameness, where no one unique characteristic or trait plays a role. Identity means also both something that apply to one human being seen externally and only that, and something that concerns groups and masses.

The concept of the personality has gone out of style, resulting in confusion for those who attempt to find a clearer picture of self. Should they look for something that pertains only to their inner reality, or should they strive to develop all they have in common with their type and that determines their different memberships?

We often talk about gender identity, about nationality, class identity, etc. These are the equality or conformity concepts. They describe the masses, groups, behavior and roles, the impersonal, outer or social characteristics. For example, developing gender identity means to conform and adapt to the norms that apply to one's own gender, whether this concerns mental, physical or practical characteristics and tasks. Gender identity, and other mass identities, can mean loss of personality and be caused by self-annihilation.

Mass identity concepts are almost always political. They are connected to domestic/national or international modifications. National identity is initiated once a country is liberated or engaged in a war. Racial identity gains meaning when an oppressed group gains independence or when the group is oppressed even more. For a long time, the concept of gender identity was used to prevent women from getting an education and from participating in professional life or politics. In our day, the concept has been used to unite women against men and as argument for women's rights to power and influence.

Naturally, there are times in life when it can be important to identify with a mass especially if an individual is not sure in what group where he or she really belongs. In times of political crisis, one needs clear lines in order to avoid difficulties. Group attachment is a protection, a membership in an alliance.

But in times of peace, in times of awakening, mass identity becomes a boomerang. In times of women's liberations, if the goal is to liberate the personal, idealizing gender identity will prevent liberation and only serve to fortify the battle between the rival gender groups. As a rule, each mass movement will often destroy precisely what they need. As *Ortega* says: "In revolts caused by hunger, the mob usually demands bread, in that end it wrecks the bakeries."[21] Liberation movements will therefore often attack the personal and personalities.

Identity on the mass level will always threaten the development of the person and the personality. The personality is the expression of the person, and shows his or her distinctive character and unique experiences of existence, it is unique for this person compared to the other. The personality is embedded in humanity, precisely in that which is one's consciousness and subjectivity. Via the personality the human being, becomes its own eyewitness, and understands that it is the only eyewitness to both its own existence and inner reality.

We need to understand the personality in the starting point, as *Miguel de Unamuno* does: "There is no other "I" in the world. This is a thought we must never forget, . . . but most especially do not forget that when they come to us with all that nonsense about being an atom in the universe and that without us the stars will still follow their course, and that the good will survive without our help and that it is self-deception to believe that the world was created for us. There is no other "I" in the world. Each of us is unique and cannot be replaced by another. Each of us is absolute. . . Others can be as great or less, better or worse, but there is no other "I." I am something completely new. An eternity of pasts is woven together in me, and from me will arise an eternity of the future. There is no other "I."[22]

Each 'I' is different from all other 'I's'. Each of us has a name of our own, a signature for us and us alone. This name is revealed through inner reality when experiencing existence, through seeing and hearing, being seen and heard, being visible and distinct. This name is the experience and the experience is the name. The person is a whole world.

The experience of the self has no parallel with another for anyone. It is its own moving, changeable substance. The personality is always something dynamic, something living. From this comes the unique, what each person has alone, him or herself.

The personality is like new life, with innate possibilities, in principle not lucidity, implies development and first and foremost an organic whole. It is like a river that finds its way in unknown territory, expanding and crating.

The personality is not shaped by society, by groups and crowds, nor is it shaped only through the need to be different; it is not created by man. Rather, it is discovered and developed through the ability to express the personal, let oneself grow up, and mature.

Each can naturally nurture and develop his or her personality, but only within the framework that actually is offered. And diversity will always force new choices, new forms for personal expression.

It is from our experience of inner reality that we can see that the personality is real, while (mass) identity is a work of man and forced through from society. These are forms that people are pressured to or choose to take on. But this is the picture as seen from the person.

The experience of identity and personality will be totally different if the starting point is the mass man/woman or the individual.

The mass man/woman will, if they seek their own personality, instead find inner emptiness, confusion, and stereotypes. For this they will try to compensate. The inner emptiness can only be compensated by a successful life in the center of the crowd. In all likelihood mass man/woman will not understand the question or the longing for an inner world. This will be viewed as mysticism or some kind of hysteria and dismissed, and reject it with "not" "shuddering" at the thought of being exactly like everyone else.

To the contrary, it will regard their memberships as important and real. When it feels like someone, it is because it feels like someone with a right to a membership and fills the criteria for membership, perhaps better than all the others. Each has the special something that makes him or her, for example, part of the English aristocracy, an African-American from Harlem, a true German, a real man or a real woman. And it knows this and appreciates it.

The individual will also experience emptiness in the inner lives. But it will try to fill that emptiness by leaving all groups and transfer to the outer reality what can only be found in the inner. The inner uniqueness is lost because the individual wants to transform it into the experience of others. The individual can't stand to experience his/her uniqueness alone.

But if the individual is unable to experience of the internal, he/she is constantly longing for it, and search for it everywhere in outer surroundings.

Because of its isolation, it has a real need for an inner reality, a secret room, and a possibility for escape should the outside world not confirm the need to be unique, something above the others. As a result, it creates for itself a false inner world, one filled with daydreams, feats, honors and distinctions, or with defeat, depending on the goal for the lives. Often any means can be used that make it feel different from all others.

Therefore, the inner world of the individual will also be static. This is so especially if the individual does not succeed in getting recognition for its difference from everyone else, if the mass does not experience him or her as a contrasting individual. The disgust for the mass never reaches such a degree that the individual doesn't need to use the public or need a public. Between the mass and the individual there is a truce; both needs the other in order to define themselves and their role.

Both mass man and the individual can readily experience the dynamic and changeable inner reality as a threat, should they ever gain a glimpse of it. The mass man/woman will see the demand to individualize themselves; the individual will see the threat from the society and the need to subjugate to others. The fact that existence can change so quickly is viewed as dangerous; it creates insecurity and problems, shapes a chaos in which only persons can find meaning and wholeness.

Chapter IV

Interpersonal Room

WHEN WE OBSERVE HUMAN relationships from outside, we see small and large groups formed and dissolved. These are called networks. Some networks are more established and stable than others, such as family and kinfolk. Others come and go through our participation in a career, politics, sports, cultural and religious forums as well as relationships with friends. Many are open to anybody. Some networks, such as sects and secret societies, are closed absolutely. Some offer a great deal of freedom to the individual members, while some dictate strict rules for behavior and lifestyle.

There are many different networks: societies, organizations, institutions, clubs, lodges, gangs, circles, associations, guilds, alliances, brotherhoods, federations, juntas, coalitions, corporations, fraternities, unions. . .

To be human is literally to always be a *member*; we are always enrolled, no matter whether we are active or passive. Networks too are our partners, even when the conditions can seem somewhat diffuse.

In social life we will quickly been draw into networks and committed by our memberships. We can easily become a mass man/woman, without realizing it. In order to attain success, we must play our part well, but as actors of daily life we become easily replaced. If we don't want to find ourselves in the periphery or become an outsider, we increase our performance. That is why social life, and the need for it, is the biggest threat against the personal.

Insight into social patterns can be of great help while developing as a person. When we become aware of the various possible networks, we can begin to choose among them while learn about their members. We can learn that no one shares their inner reality with others, except during special moments, and that everyone is vulnerable in their uniqueness. There is a chance that personal relationships can develop.

When networks call upon the mass man/woman inside us, or provoke the individual in us, we do not need to respond. The response can be the personal, as possible and as relevant as we are able to.

Networks: Consequences and Confusion

Networks surround us and protect us from a chaotic world and our own loneliness. By getting to know some networks, we can gain insight into others, and leave at least some of them behind and join new ones.

Any time we are around people, whether at a meeting, on a bus, streetcar, train or plane, in waiting rooms, at a hotel, at restaurants, in shops, at parties, or just passing on the street, we find ourselves in a network. In our society such networks are almost literally rooms; we are in rooms when we find ourselves in networks. And it is always possible to see networks as rooms, even though they can be enormous and even endless. Relationships between people, communication itself, or the lack thereof, can be experienced as all that takes place within the boundaries of time and space, decidedly here and now.

Visualizing networks as rooms can also help fix our attention on what is here and now and helps us analyze the rooms we find ourselves in on a daily basis. With this as our frame of reference, we are better able to gain a glimpse of both the inner and outer factors that can either confuse or help communication. We can better distinguish between what and who plays a role; it isn't always necessarily how we in advance had thought it would be.

Some of the features of the rooms will have a greater effect on us than others and seem decisive, and determining, for the communication that can be realized. It is the possibility for dialogue that determines whether the room is suitable for the personal.

A. The purely *physical* quality of the room will be one such feature. The development of cities and objects, *exteriors*, landscapes, character, can all affect people's relationships to each other and interaction. Nature also plays a role in how receptive and open people are. The lines between exteriors and interiors are blurred depending on how space is defined and whether several spaces can be experienced at once. Outside your own home, there is a street, a town, a district, a country, a continent, a planet, and the cosmos. ...

Interiors play a significant role when considering the possibilities for and limits to communication. We are affected one way when surrounded by antiques and quite another when surrounded by plastic furniture and paper plates. Cafeterias influence us differently than churches and cathedrals. All interiors help form our consciousness and demonstrate the status of our activities. Old-fashioned schools exhibit a different attitude towards knowledge than modern schools; old jails or hospitals indicate different attitudes towards crime and sickness than the modern buildings. These old rooms are witnesses to discipline and subjugation, hierarchy and absolute authority, while the new ones reveal something about fellowship and openness as well as fluid roles and chaos.

Urbanites and country folk, aristocrats and commoners, and many other types, usually suit their surroundings, suit the spaces they have furnished and the objects they have chosen for their daily encounters. We resemble the exteriors and the interiors we choose and in which we thrive the best, and the other way around. Not least of all, it is difficult to imagine conversations in middle class environments without the overabundance in the dwellings, with all the small chairs, the pleasant lighting and nick knacks. This ornamentation is well suited to their conversations and the absence of the personal.

B. We can also describe the interpersonal room as it relates to *psychological* qualities. It can be described by referring to human proximity and distance, openness and impassivity, moods and atmosphere, waves and vibrations, or power struggles and intrigues.

In modern environments, dominated by psychoanalysis and skepticism, there will for instance be openness where sexuality and feelings in relationship to family and the past are concerned, but not about deeper values and emotions. In Christian groups and families, the opposite would likely be the case.

C. A third important component is the *cognitive*, rational, logical and factual level of propositions in the room or the group.

We can describe the room by finding out which propositions are accepted as truth without any justification or argumentation, and which are automatically accepted as false.

We can also discover leaks in our thinking, areas that are not tried out, neither by idle talk nor in debates. Here, we will often find profound metaphysical beliefs of the type that are considered so obviously true or false about reality and people's place in it that it is unnecessary to either prove or disprove them.

The space creates boundaries not only for conversation and debate but also for thought and perception. Our experience of reality is governed by our understanding and reason. Some boundaries are so fundamental that only people from other cultures and environments will be able to perceive them, we ourselves will always take them for granted. The eye of the beholder can determine not only what will be seen but also its form.

D. Not least of all, the room's *moral code* is the decisive component for the degree of openness and inaccessibility to communication. How one should behave, or what is allowed to be said and done, can be strictly regulated. The lines of tolerance are widely varying depending on which interpersonal circumstances and groups one inhabits.

It is in this arena that we can find the most frequent collisions with the personal. Some new, unexpected, or very difficult moral thought will force people out of their roles, get them to take a stand, declare an opinion, and perhaps also to confront other people.

E. While the next component may be easier to understand, it can be complicated to see its effects. *Social* categories place a clear limit on the possibilities for self-expression and meeting others. The composition of gender, age, class, race, socio- economic status, and prestige drives the conversation and determines the outcome.

Groups entirely of women, for instance of mothers of small children, have very specific themes in their conversations that often is difficult to get through. Groups of business professionals have very different themes, but the conversations are just as limited.

F. The next important component is the *economic*, in a wide sense of concept. In any group, some kind of trading occurs. We can describe what we ourselves contribute and what we receive return. In the interpersonal space, may a thousand goods being contributed and received, ranging from time, attention, friendliness, politeness, money, food and drink, a good place to sit, exciting themes, psychic energy, and the will to get to know others. Some people give more often while others wait until they have received something they think is of value. The scope of the gifts determines also the possibility for communication as well as the character.

G. One last component I will mention is the *creative* scope of the interpersonal space. Does the foundation allow a place for whimsy, spontaneity, and renewal? If that is the case, then it is functioning creatively. If there is nothing but routine, habits, and repetition, there can be little creativity, but rather stagnation, and likely for some members of the group, deep frustration. The personal cannot be expressed without allowing some room for the new and the unexpected.

Many of these features, and some others that are not mentioned, could easily blend into one another, and in practice it may not be so easy to distinguish one from the other. Some components are more important than others where open or closed communication, information, and conversation are concerned.

The main thing is to be aware of the obstacles that exist for communicating. There is no point in banging the head against the wall. If some interpersonal spaces are difficult it may be possible to make some changes. If not, then one must realize that the only option is to get out of the group as quickly as possible. In fact, many problems with communicating are due largely to the fact that participants do not try to understand the interpersonal space in which they find themselves.

With your attention directed towards the group as a whole and the conditions of the space, one should be able to improve one's own situation and relationships to other people. One should be discriminating in relating to the interpersonal, just as important as in one's choice of friends and partners.

Naturally it isn't possible to automatically apply ready-made analyses. Analyses are retrospective, created by thoughtful reflection. In the moment of experiencing something, intuition plays a more important role. That too will usually be insufficient. The essential reason for this is the magnitude and chaos of the moment. Only the correct balance of reflection and intuition can help you find space for the personal. Expressing yourself demands both discernment and the ability to act spontaneously. Both analyses and intuition must bow to the magnitude and decisive power of the moment.

Everyday Reality

Let me change perspectives and take a look at the interpersonal from within, even from the middle. From this "in the middle of" perspective comes *daily life*. Also in the middle of daily experiences, a structure appears, or perhaps the lack thereof, that can tell us something about the possibilities and challenges of the personal.

A. The first thing you will notice is chaos and variety. From the lack of a better word, everyday reality has to be understood as *pre-scientific*. In our daily lives there are feelings, intuitions, premonitions, and senses that have enormous meaning. The human being who is best able to organize these experiences will become successful and get the most out of existence. One should be able to "swing" with the flow without drowning in the complexity.

Everyday life leaves little room for doubt, investigations, observations, or theories. It is too near or too real for that. It is important to stress that this is not a fault or something that can become different. In daily life, reality is experienced directly; all of science and theories are derived.

In many ways, daily life is, therefore, the domain of creative people. In the world of science and professional arts, the creative is often the result of method and craft; that is the creative has been put into a system.

The creative and clear thought can truly exist only in daily life. Thinking clearly clarifies chaos. As Ortega says: "The man who is capable of steering a clear course,... who can perceive under the chaos presented by every vital situation the hidden anatomy of the movement, the man, in a word, who does not lose himself in life, he is in truth the man with a clear head."[23]

Those who can live within the reality of daily life, take in and relate to its entirety will have a great deal more reality of emotion and thought than theoreticians, whether they are philosophers, artists, social scientists, or politicians. It is not first of all the theories that get in the way, but the artificial clarity of those theories.

B. It is precisely this chaos in daily life that can and must create *prejudices*. No one can absorb everything, and no one can avoid feeling anxious about the chaos from time to time. No one can always understand nor like everything and everyone, nor allow everyone to have a chance.

Prejudices, comes from *pre*understanding and *pre*-judgment. In advance of experiences there are ideas about experiences. These preconceived notions are multi-faceted. They serve largely as traffic rules regarding our behavior, accepted practices, food, drink, and view of humanity, their actions and work. Preferences change from one environment to another. Some fashions and trends, are easily changed, we ditch a preference if we find it useful and opportune to do so. Other preferences are more general and bound by tradition.

Prejudices can be understood as something positive. They become a defense against chaos; their task is to simplify and organize so that daily life is easier, unambiguous, and well arranged. Prejudices helps by offering safety and security in a world that does not offer much of that.

The use of prejudices one can further cultivate oneself and one's own people; prejudices about the colored made whites whiter; prejudices regarding men made women even more Madonna-like. We have to have rules that cause us to assume that we like some people, that some are better than others, and the other way around. If we do not have these rules, we can drown in all the possibilities and have so many friends and people to deal with that we are suffocated by demands and responsibilities. It is necessary to be able to say that this is not my concern, and to be able to simplify the world in daily life.

Prejudices also enable us to perceive of and plan for a future, so that we can choose when realistically, when not having the time or possibility for any analysis. Through the help of bias, we have no need to engage once again in every phenomenon and every person we meet. Prejudices solve many problems for us and helps protect us against what may be unexpected and unpredictable.

But prejudices can also be perceived as negative. They prevent openness, renewal, and excess. Through simplifying daily life, they can also trivialize it, make it seem ordinary and set in its ways, and in the final analysis, make it seem unreal. When everything is as expected, the meaning of experiencing itself disappears, and new experiences become impossible. Therefore, it can be said that prejudices prevent life experiences of a more fundamental and necessary type.

Prejudices are also negative in the way they impact human beings; prejudices are often the reason that people do not receive the justice or the social rights to which they have a right, and inflict wounds such as prison and punishment, deportation and displacement.

Negative prejudices are also boomerangs; they always harm those who have them. Those who are prejudiced have weakened their sense of reality, and they remain in a daily life full of illusions and delusions.

The ability to see this ambiguity of bias can be an aid when attempting to choose at least some of them with more care and concern.

In general, mass man will have the most obvious biases, those that are normal in the group or milieu. While the individual will have certain fixations, the person will have the fewest and most neutral biases. As a result, the work for new possibilities for the person is also a work for greater understanding in the interpersonal.

C. Another similar rule of the road we often use is *taste differs*. Taste is therefore an important feature in our understanding of daily life.

Taste is perhaps the most obvious expression of the individual. It cannot be appealed and will not be discussed. It is all encompassing, applying just as much to what we truly know about as to that about which we know nothing at all and have no experience.

Taste is often the basis for people's decisions about what is esthetic and ethically good or bad. The good, the individual believe is what he/she likes and desires, and bad is all that they do not like. Taste is therefore the first and foremost a sign the individual has decided on something. Because of this decision, he/she can say with certainty this I like, this I don't like. And since the individual only see itself in the world, its taste is the same thing as a final judgment.

D. Taste is not the determining factor for the person. *Evaluation* is central. Evaluation is reflection, results from insight into the complexity and variety of phenomena and through knowledge. While taste often is usually concerned with familiarity to a phenomenon without knowledge, evaluation is acquaintance with many phenomena as well as common knowledge.

Insight both into form, content, and context produces evaluation. With evaluation arise an integration of the prescientific into daily life and taste.

A real connoisseur is experienced, accomplished, and well educated. He or she is also able to disregard fashions and expectations and perceive the new and unexpected in phenomena. The evaluation is spontaneous and deals with the object directly. The decision about what is good or bad can been made on a solid foundation. Evaluation means transcending and expanding. The knowing being, understands continually more, and add new phenomena to the view of the world. In evaluation our analysis and intuition are united and developed simultaneously.

Naturally, there are often transitional areas between bias, taste and evaluation. They can affect each other in many contexts. The more primitive we are, or have to be, the more we need to depend on our biases and our taste. The more mature we are, and the more that reality gives us the possibility to grow, the more we can cultivate our ability to judge. Mass man makes use of bias and in so doing nullifies the possibility for plurality. The individual thinks in terms of taste and preferences and can therefore also find a path in chaos, while simultaneously the biases can become less substantive.

Squarely in the middle of the interpersonal space we must continually engage with chaos and multitude. We have to learn to relate to this, so that we are not totally overwhelmed or exhausted by all we can experience. The lack of order in daily life is the most important challenge that all people face. If we are unable to find a true order, we must at least be able to imagine that there is such a thing.

Our prejudices, taste and preferences, or reason, of necessity will dominate communication and decide what possibilities there are for expression of the personal.

Only by using evaluation can we engage the personal and create vital and honest communication in our interpersonal space. If the first step is to express prevailing biases, and the second is to express your likes or dislikes, then the third step is to clarify and bring oneself and ones experiences into the conversation so that there is an opening for general insights, and an invitation to others for shared subjectivity.

These are the norms that dominate communication and daily life, whether we have developed our relationship to our inner world or not, and whether we live our lives as mass man, individual, or person.

Doubt and Faith

Modern men don't appear to like themselves much. They are often controlled by feelings that isolate and depress. If we are to judge by divorce and health statistics, there are many who live in difficult situations.

The dominant feeling of the times seems to be *paranoia*. Groups exert pressure by expressing distrust and displaying vigilance. Some groups clearly have adversaries who they almost by definition do not trust; the masses and their rival masses dominate our culture with their monotonous declarations of distrust. Members of Labor Party oppose members of the Conservative Party, Humanists oppose Christians, women's groups oppose perceived male dominated society, homosexuals oppose heterosexuals, and so on. Suspicion sours the public debate. Many see it as their mission to expose and condemn and in one way or another punish individuals from rival groups.

One explanation for this can be that in these modern times, relationships between people are often disposable or exploitative.[24] Modern men seem to distrust people in general, and don't believe any longer in others or themselves as loving and generous. On the other hand, people do seem to believe in the welfare society, the state, consumption, equality, things, and roles.

Another explanation for this can be the influence of scientific thought during the last hundred years. This type of thinking holds that nothing can be true until it has been proven or for other reasons accepted as true. People who want to be considered modern think scientifically and, as a result, doubt systematically. But if doubt has an important function in science, it becomes destructive when inserted into the interpersonal. When cynical positions focus attention on what is negative and evil, and seldom on what is good, then people are doomed to be discontented with themselves. Whatever pulls us down has a strange value of its own; cynicism is often dogmatic.

The Scottish philosopher *John Macmurray* puts his finger on something essential when he states: "The method of doubt rests upon an assumption, which should be made explicit, that a reason is required for believing but none for doubting. . . If I find myself possessed of a certain belief, and know no reason for questioning it, I *cannot* doubt it; and if I could my doubt would be irrational. Moreover, if I do doubt one of my beliefs, then it is no longer a belief of mine, but only something that I used to believe."[25]

There are characteristics about these daily experiences that we have every day that run contrary to conventional doubt and paranoia and show that ordinary cognition has to build upon something other than cynical doubt. Daily life underscores our enormous ability for faith and trust. Even the most doubting philosopher, humanist, and skeptic cannot do otherwise than to base their 'here and now' life on faith and confidence.

In daily life, doubt is really a façade while faith becomes increasingly inclusive in the future. It simply is not possible to live today without faith and trust. It is the ability to believe that makes daily life livable and makes it possible to survive with our reason intact.

This is closely connected to how specialized modern society has become and people's accompanying ignorance and lack of education in the majority of arenas. In time there will be no experts; just a few people, if any, can have sufficient oversight of their specialties. Most people will live with large gaping holes in their knowledge and thought. Real experts don't longer exist, and we will be more and more dependent on each other and left to chance.

Each day we *have* to trust our surroundings. Our kitchens and homes are full of electrical apparatuses we neither understand nor can deal with should there be an accident. The same goes for means of transportation. There are few drivers or passengers on streetcars, buses, planes or trains know anything about motors and their construction or know how they should behave should any problems arise while traveling. Most of us have accordingly no command over the apparatuses that we use every day.

That same impotence dominates when we have ailing bodies. Medical knowledge remains the domain of doctors, dentists and others in that profession. Mental problems have to be handled by psychologists or psychiatrists. Anytime there is something wrong with us, no matter what, we are completely dependent on other people's knowledge, ability, and will to help us.

Our food supply shows our total dependence perhaps better than anything else. Food and drink contain large quantities of chemicals that we know nothing about. We are completely dependent on strangers to show responsibility and discernment on our behalf.

Our global energy supply also clearly exhibits our vulnerability; we are forced to trust that the energy we use is not harmful and that it is available when we need it. Modern technological society is frighteningly fragile.

In the same way, we are weak and dependent in our careers and welfare lives. We have to trust that state and municipal authorities will come should we need any help, only a few people are members of natural, caring networks. The state has become our great mother and father who support and take care of us, when we in some area or other cannot help ourselves. All demands must be directed to the state. We have to trust the politicians both at home and abroad, the judicial system, the police and defense departments, and the common sense of the secret service.

The digital age can only increase our helplessness and vulnerability, and places even greater demands on our faith and trust. The more we live in an incomprehensible and complicated world, the more we need to develop our ability to trust. And this trust is alpha and omega for our harmony.

As a result, it is not just a little ironic that cynicism and paranoia has become so prevalent. But what is happening could well be a reprioritization of the content of faith. Faith in the state, technology and rationality has replaced faith in divine powers to the point of irrationality.

Modern society considers faith in God and the holy as irrational superstition, but has no problem accepting people's blind faith in society itself. Despite all the car, plane, and atomic power plant accidents; fires; acts of violence; sickness; murder and suicide—not to mention the constantly documented disagreements and incompetence of experts from many places—there are few to none who have begun some kind of campaign to increase doubt in modern society. Criticism is directed for the most part towards separate occurrences. Even socialists and communists, who are otherwise very good at pointing out crises, have not yet realized that modern society is in many ways one continuous crisis. Fundamental doubt is always rejected. Modern society stands unshaken; in reality humanity believes in itself and its society as if it were God, himself.

Modern people are therefore only ostensibly filled with suspicion and doubt. In reality, they are permeated by a faith so strong that perhaps no one before has experienced anything like it. They live in an everyday mechanized faith that affects their entire existence. But this is concealed.

Let me illustrate the modern human being with a story about Joey.[26] Joey, an autistic American boy of 8 was convinced that he was a machine. Each day, for every task, he had to be "plugged" into an electrical outlet, whether it was for sleeping, eating, or using the toilet. Joey had built an ingenuous system to ensure that he always had a cable that he could connect himself to do any job that he wanted. The personnel who took care of him had to accept all of his wires and plugs and the view of him as a machine in order to be able to take care of him.

In a way, one can say that Joey was obsessed by a radical doubt in himself. He couldn't do anything himself without help from outside. Even the most basic actions had to be regulated and supervised by mechanical equipment. Without what he associated with electricity, he was helplessly lost. He viewed himself as an incubator-baby.

It is also just as possible to say that Joey had the ability to experience a strong and absolute faith. He believed in a machine he had created himself. He was of course no electrician! Instead of depending on his own human powers, he believed in his creation: the machine.

Joey's story is interesting. First of all, it illustrates something about all the demands a truly doubting human being places on his or her surroundings; it was the others who had to connect Joey to the machine and guide him through the many dangers of the day. Secondly, and more importantly in this situation, these others had to have a faith and trust in Joey, faith that he would himself have denied the possibility of should he have been able to understand it. Where he had no belief in the life inside him, the others had to believe, even when he through his behavior had declared himself to be a dead machine. Their faith was what also made him well.

But the third point is the most important. Joey's doubt in himself could only be paralleled to the enormous faith he had in the machine, and both were just as irrational. His doubt in himself was completely irrational, as his faith in electricity. Is it possible that irrational doubt can only be overcome through irrational faith?

Joey is, as mentioned, in many ways a perfect picture of the modern man. Their complete doubt in all that it is rational to believe in, such as the divine, the holy, the innate mystery of existence, self, body and soul, other people and the interpersonal space, has brought with it a belief in all that is rational to doubt, such as doubt itself, technology, analysis, the state, and the incapacitated human being.

Faith in God and the holy has been transferred to the phenomena and the values on which modern man is deeply dependent. Modern faith is therefore far more irrational that the ancient faith in the gods; in reality a process of primitivism has occurred, of both people and their religion. People have become incubator babies, and instead of seeing the Divine in objects, they see the objects as divine. In a daily life that consists of endless amounts of small disasters, modern human beings believe in that which has caused all these breakdowns.

In other words, doubt and faith are fundamental, central categories in our daily life and our perception of daily life. It is easy to think that these categories are eternal and universal expressions for different human phases.

Mass man has little to no ability for any other faith other than this modern superstition; it believes in the society it has created, in its groups, biases and tastes, technology, and the state. First and foremost, it believes in the ordinary, and that everything is, as it seems. It has nothing but disdain for the uncommon and is not even able doubt the existence of God. God, the absolute and universal plays absolutely no role in its life. We can't say that mass man is really able to doubt because it takes everything for granted, that things are what they seem to be. Mass man lives in a state of true superstition.

The individual on the other hand are consumed by doubt, except periodically in him/herself. Their self-confidence is gladly reversed proportional to the lack of confidence in others. Just like mass man, the individual thrust technology if it suits it's self-image as outsider and rebel. The individual trusts his/her own powers and expected accomplishments. On the other hand, others are always insignificant in their eyes. Should others believe that they too are meaningful, they are mistaken. For the individual, all others are just beings; they themselves are the only "I." The individual is desperate, to make him /herself immortal.

The *person* naively and confidently believes in universal values, the holy, friendship, love and communication, other people's strengths and possibilities while doubting modern society, the state, and technical rationality. The person relates directly to reality, consciously and judiciously. At the same time, he or she does not worry too much about daily life. A life where the human being is self-sufficient as much as possible becomes most desirable. The goal is to master at least some of the situations that one can encounter. That all must at times often be lost in modern society is obvious.

Through the help of these two categories: doubt and faith, we can also describe two widely different pictures of reality. These pictures are interchangeable in us, depending on our phase and existential choices.

The world of *faith* is a good, true, and beautiful place. It is a living whole, has both depth and width, and is transcendent. It unites and reconciles, builds bridges, shows possibilities and connections between opposites. Faith has its own safety. It is its own truth.

At the same time it is also demanding, and the human being must resign to something that is greater, more and different from him/herself. Humility and the ability to serve and to adapt are necessary.

The world of *doubt,* is divided, disharmony continually threatens to completely take over. It is unorganized, dark, chaotic, and full of excluding opposites. Besides being joyless, dutiful, conventional, and meaningless in itself, it is often full of lies and falsehood. Nothing is as it seems. The world of doubt consists of many small puzzle pieces one can strive to put together for a whole life, and still not arrive at a meaningful picture.

At the same time one has elbowroom to believe whatever one wants to believe; he/she can control reality, according to their needs, desires, definitions, technologies and language. One lives freely in the empty room.

While the person has the inclination to believe, mass man and the individual have the tendency to doubt. While mass man doubts the unique, the exceptional, and the singular, the individual doubts relationships and fellowship, not at least those in private life and close relations.

The modern human being can only be optimistic about technology and skeptical rationality. Because technology is impersonal, already outside of the sphere of the person, faith in technology becomes an enormous victory over the personal. Technology can fulfill the dream of quantitative equality and justice.

Because our society has discarded faith, faith is not understood, and the person is not accepted. Therefore, the metaphysical, religious and personal reality becomes the number one object of doubt. The ones who doubt everything that is worth believing in, march onward, believing in all that they should doubt.

Onward also marches a society that honors skeptics, cynics, persecutors, and nihilists and their political ideologies, while all who believe in something other than the modern technological welfare society, who strive to express the personal, are unhappy and miserable.

Onward also marches a picture of leaders and modern gods. Our gods need to have the characteristic features of technology, rationality, the state, and the welfare society. They must illustrate their belief that people are encased in incubators, deeply dependent upon machines, and essentially viewed as weak and helpless beings. Political leaders tell people that they will have more things, steadily assuring them that their essential and necessary needs will be taken care of by the state. While luxury and unnecessary goods people will be allowed to get for themselves. The ideal seems to be a supported population that just works to earn some spending money. The people, becomes like spoiled teenagers, and the state like the rich parent who has long since given up on their offspring but continue to keep them alive.

The only optimistic part of this picture is the human being's real ability to *believe*. Even though the gods are false and have feet of clay, an unseen faith shows that there is life and hope. The strength in the power of faith shows that the human being is something other than he/she realize. If the human being only wake up to its own faith and becomes conscious of it, there is hope that he/she could also see that the dance around the state as mechanical mother is not worth the faith, but points towards a far more worthy goal.

This faith can hide Christianity; but it can also hide faith in the personal and the person, and in the fact that people themselves are full of innate possibilities, freedom, and responsibility.

Negative and Positive Symbols

The interpersonal is our daily life. We continually find ourselves in many different rooms. They are the constant factors, despite changes, variety and unwieldiness.

The interpersonal exposes us to influences and stimulation. At times, it is extremely difficult to gain an impression of the value of what is happening around us. The power of the interpersonal often depends on our ignorance of what is happening and the place where we live.

These rooms are revealed mainly through symbols. The symbols evoke strong, emotional reactions without necessarily having any basis in reality. This is elementary. But what isn't elementary is the fact that symbols often guide our lives, and our lives are often determined by something that doesn't come from us or other living beings and their realities, but quite simply from symbols.

It is also not elementary that such powerful symbols can have a direct hypnotic effect on us, making us into somebody other than who we usually are. Symbols often influence our most irrational and diffuse feelings. We can be blown around like leaves in the wind if a symbol has a strong effect on us. We can suddenly get caught up in a situation we would never have believed possible. In different forms of mass suggestion and gang mentality, we can clearly recognize this. The most insignificant can become leaders, the weak become our commanders, and the strong succumb. Symbols influence even the isolated.

We are constantly subjected to suggestive symbols. As long as there are conventional symbols, it can be impossible to understand how much they transform us. Knowing that, we need to break their power over us and become influenced by something else that is more important and real.

We are also dependent on our ability to locate and understand symbols, and to be able to distinguish between negative and positive symbols, letting ourselves be guided by what we believe is valuable. There is little use in describing and distinguishing between symbols in theory if we are unable to recognize what symbols affect us in practice.

A symbol can be many different things; objects, actions, words, relationships, anything that can elicit emotions and action from the one affected, whether this occurs in fellowship with others or in isolation. This is why it is generally impossible to make a classification of symbols. But each of us should be able to gain some insight into symbols by analyzing the interpersonal and things that have happened. The criteria are whether we feel affected by something or someone, pulled in a specific direction, more or less against our will. Symbols can be anything from the flag and the national anthem, to pictures and soulful melodies. Private symbols create most of the difficulties, especially those connected to the unconscious and the archetypal. These are certainly the most loaded.

Fertile and positive symbols are based in interpersonal realities, in the personal sphere. They work from powers that do not veil or transform the space and the participants. They strengthen, clarify, and elucidate what is already present in the people and the circumstances.

In many ways, these symbols create better spaces and allow nuances with more dimensions. They expand minds and the conversation. They make things better, build on all that has capacity for life and health, and make it all real. Through positive symbols we are able to express what we actually feel and believe; they help us to present ourselves as we are, to recognize and remember ourselves.

The snow-covered mountain plateaus during Easter holidays remind one of eternity and peace. A beautifully set table can make us remember the importance of a confidential and intimate conversation, a gift can tell us about the love we feel.

Negative and destructive symbols do not reflect interpersonal space. They insert something new; hate where no hate has been before, love that does not exist. They revamp individuals and relationships between them in the same way narcotics and alcohol can influence and change someone, or ideologies and religious opinions can blind someone. Negative symbols will, over time, more or less take control of the individual. The individual steps into the service of something else, becomes a slave of the symbols and directly dependent on them. Just as the uniform gives a military idealizer the feeling that he is the one that is visible and distinct, compared to civilians, which to him seems naked and stupid.

Mass man and the individual would rather not be themselves, rather not live their own personal lives. They are happy to accept transforming symbols. They are intoxicated by them and let the symbols structure their lives. When they cling to symbols, their inner emptiness is filled by feelings. Negative symbols provide a sense of reality where there is none.

Mass man seeks symbols that nullify any individuality, anything that makes him or her more like others, and anything that comes from others. Mass man seeks to fill the self with whatever the others have so that he or she can feel like somebody. The purpose of the individual's transforming symbols is to make him or her stand out from others. The individual seeks to establish his or her exceptionality through surface characteristics.

Naturally there can be fluid boundaries between positive and negative symbols. One of the reasons for this is the need for self-deceit, since the negative symbols often act on deeply subconscious, primitive feelings, repressions, and inhibitions. Because of lack of reality in people, their shadow world, their attraction for the negative, these symbols can seem real.

Just as it is difficult in our living human reality to distinguish between the collective, the individual, and the personal it can also be difficult to distinguish between positive and negative symbols. This discrimination also depends on the fundamental life choices people make.

Emotions and Ideals

Anyone who has traveled the road from mental illness to wellness has managed to get rid of some damaging symbols. As a result, there is a possibility for increased clarity for most of us. We can find one criterion in our feelings and ideals.

Our emotions can often seem hollow. If we pay close attention, we can sense that they don't resonate within us or within our interpersonal room. We can sense our false, inauthentic feelings the same way as we can hear false tones.

In conventional situations, we can hear how hollow chitchat and common phrases really are. Everyone thinks it is *so* nice to get together, all you are saying is *so* important, it is *so* great to get together. Compliments fit the situation, or the party, and we say what should be said. This doesn't need to be negative; the use of words depends on their purpose, words are actions that set the scene. The purpose is to stabilize and fortify the relationship. Not to use the phrases will destroy the character of the company. If you have no need for a closer relationship, it is foolish to try to give the gathering a different content. Within the conventional, there are values worth keeping, like giving people a place in a network that can be useful in special situations.

In this way, all of our words, actions and choices are bound together with emotions. When emotions reverberate, they feel real, you can tell by how unobtrusive they are and they emerge without any outer pressure or artificial stimuli. They just are there, and you know that they have roots in something that is valuable in and of itself in other people, in relationships, nature, art, and all that we connect with the divine.

True emotions connect us to something that is permanent, universal, and absolute. Those emotions that strengthen our personalizing values, that strengthen the good, the true, and the beautiful are far much more real than those that can't.

These true emotions come into being from meeting with living reality. They emerge in those living with an internally driven honesty and desire to know who they are, even when this hurts can destroy someone's self-image.

Or when what is worthwhile intrude on you, so you are forced to acknowledge it in yourself; the 'aha' feelings arise.

This also means that false emotions can contain elements of reality that conceal emotions that you don't realize you have. Intense aggression may conceal weakness; ecstasy may be a cover for emptiness, forced joy for depression, and depression may hide sorrow. Many emotions may be of a duel or complex nature. The false emotions may be subject to misinterpretation because of a strong wish to feel something special. If someone has a real desire to be married, it is easy to imagine being in love.

In order to distinguish between what is real and what is false, positive and negative, we can also analyze familiar values and ideals. This can be especially helpful in times of emotional confusion.

Once again, what is real is part of the ordinary and personal. We must continually choose ideals that link us to reality and allow us to find our place in a transcending connection. Materialist, economic, and short-term values and ideals like those that put our focus on career and social status will expose us to negative symbols and depreciate our quality of life. Overemphasis on values of these kinds binds us to a reality that is dead and lacks perspective, they do not point outside themselves.

If one reflects on one's values, one can also make oneself clearer as person. Through the perseverance of our thoughts we are able to mine the gold we carry inside, find out what we are really worth, and what we stand for.

We can test our emotions and values through reflected actions. By changing habits and patterns of behavior we can more easily extract what is real in our emotions and values or gain insight into our confusion and uncertainty. In this respect false emotions are likely as daydreams, when they become real, they are not nearly as valuable as we imagined.

Positive symbols, overarching ideals and real emotions are our antennae. They help us while we are searching in the world, and they make life worth living. "What is worthwhile cannot be decided by thinking, by intellect, by science, but only by emotion. Life is an art, not a science," says *John Macmurray*.[27]

Facts, norms and values

Symbols, emotions, and ideals contribute to interpersonal multiplicity and chaos. It has consequences for the relationship between facts, norms, and values. Theoretically, there is a clear distinction between what and how things are and what and how things should be. But in the existential reality of daily life this clarity disappears and has actually never been there.

Daily life is dominated by what we consider as facts and what we consider as rules, norms and values. We are constantly making up our mind; our life is dominated by our opinions about what we have to accept and what we can regulate.

Too strong opinions about what are facts, and what is norms, how things are, and how things should be, may confuse the individual, and damage the development to the personal. When one believes in a particular set of facts, one is limited in the norms to choose between. Facts force specific choices. But those who do not acknowledge anything as facts will be taken by the emptiness and drift along. Too strong convictions about what the facts are, can blind us to variety and possibilities; while neglecting facts can result in weakening our sense of reality and loosening the grip of oneself.

In our day-to-day lives, facts and norms often coalesce; they combine and reshape one another. The movability of human beings also changes the given "objectivity." The intersubjective, is omnipresent, the countless conscious minds shield each other and reality as they simultaneously illuminate the space they have in common.

This is why facts are saturated with intentions, with the goals of different conscious minds: aspirations, dreams, wishes, plans and desires. All of these various intentions turn to facts and elevate them to that status. And this is how is should be. Only when someone's intention has been bound to something can this something gain visible meaning and become a fact to someone.

This fundamental interplay between fact and subjectivity is often forgotten. This is partly because many facts seem to be so very certain and solid that it seems absurd to claim dependence on intentions. Are facts about the weather unaffected by intentions? Only to a certain point since of course the measurements themselves are dependent upon the instruments, but whether we experience something as hot or cold depends on us. People's own body temperatures and wishes determine that. Modern nuclear physics has shown us that variety and ambiguity goes far into the world of the atom.[28]

This interplay is especially meaningful for facts about human beings, not at least about when concerning who oneself belief who one is. If a lie has been repeated often enough, one can believe in one's own wickedness, even if, in reality, one is quite the opposite, believe in one's own selflessness even if one really do nothing but manipulate others, and so on. What one believe is true about oneself becomes true whether it is true or not.

But facts about people always have a story, emerge from a specific time, and are often "accepted truths" presented as facts. Fifty years ago, there were quite different facts, for example, about the mentally handicapped than what is common today. The social contract that exists in a society demand often that agreements themselves are forgotten and therefore the choice of something as facts will be hidden from us. If one is conscious of the determining of subjectivity, there are greater possibilities to challenge and change an agreement. One is able to see the possibilities and the hope where before none could be found.

This mixture of facts and norms often determines our understanding of existence. People have a deep inclination to read directives and norms into facts. Registering something as a fact will result in the development of norms for behavior and perception. We learn from experience, as the saying goes. Facts have given us rules for everything from how to run our forestry and agriculture to our technology industries. Our experience is our teacher, not schoolbooks.

People respond to facts by adapting to them, altering behavior, sometimes for a reason, but just as often for little or no reason. Some people stop taking the subway late at night because they hear about an instance of violence. If one calls a friend and get a busy signal two or three times, one thinks that this friend must always be on the phone, so one writes a note instead. Most of the facts we experience are used as a guide, and determine the rules. All facts have this quality, and as a result facts and norms are not easily distinguished.[29]

Some facts can also single out values. The better one is to listen to what facts truly tells, recognizing the ambiguous and the variety, the better one will be able to experience and perceive underlying values. These kinds of values illustrate something about the core of the human beings, and they are often demanding.

This is probably explains why many are afraid of hearing the truth, the real facts about themselves. Facts reveal values and therefore morals and character. Values can come into direct conflict with all that people wish was present. But facts, like emotions, are created out of many layers, behind a frightening fact—a brutal truth there may be a positive value, an edifying truth. "*Facts are friendly* . . . I have perhaps been slow to coming to realize that the facts are *always* friendly. "[30]

It is natural that people want to treat facts in the light of norms and values, and the contrary. The human being is whole — perceiving, feeling, thinking, willing and acting. A good life demands one to relate actively and resolutely to facts and norms, and work to clarify the relationship between them. By this, the reality is transformed and changed, and one will gain insight into possibilities and a new future.

The Law of Interaction

The pervasive interpersonal reality, biases, opinions, discernments, symbols, emotions, ideals, norms and values, require that we think in terms of new laws and structures also when relationships between people and people's possibilities are concerned.

Usually, we think in terms of causality where the social and psychological development of a human being is concerned. Actions and fate are explained through references to the past, childhood, parents, and environment. A lot of time is spent on describing people's backgrounds. Mostly, one wants to find one definitive, triggering cause.

But thinking in terms of causality is a waste of time and distracting. Pointing out one reason for the way a life has turned out must be completely random. Why people still think in terms of causality, is connected to the emotions that causality create. By causality thinking one can be free from guilt and responsibility. A human being who looks at its life as an effect of their parents, the childhood, and so on, will also be able to view he/herself as innocent and treated unjustly by life and others.

Causality thinking also implies a degree of megalomania. It permits idealizing one self. People can become lost in their daydreams and fantasies about what they could have become had they not been stopped. Causality damages the sense of reality and call for escapism, encouraging fatalism and sentimentality.

Causality thinking cannot change anything for those who already have big troubles. However, this kind of thinking could result in someone getting even more trouble. This thinking builds up negative expectations and norms and can directly contribute to produce the will to become a loser.

It is important to realize that causes in the usual sense *don't* exist in the interpersonal. Human beings are not things. Along with every cause, lucky or unlucky, the will also operates. In the interpersonal space there exists only the subjective, including desires, life plans, dreams, wishes, fantasies; the most different intentions. In a relationship between people and choice of life-cycle, it is the will of each individual human being that determines the course. People will, choose, and act their lives. That of course does not prevent them from choosing badly or stupidly. It also does not mean that everyone has a complete grasp on what their actions can result in or where they can lead, or whether the will is just as strong in everyone.

A wish one evening of easy money, and the following act of prostitution or a bank robbery, may change the life of this human being completely. Nevertheless, prostitution, or bank robbery, was what it wanted. What was not wanted, were the consequences and the vicious cycle into which one easily is drawn by committing such actions. That some create tragedies out of their lives can be understood by the fact that they always choose the quickest and easiest action.

It is usually small acts of will, the shortsighted thoughts, convenient choices of the moment that determine a person's life, not necessarily a unifying, strong will or a choice once and for all. Few make the explicit choice to spend life in jail or to become an old whore. But they do choose each of the small steps that take them there. The life-cycle for most people is not one big step but many small ones. That can also mean that some can will self-destruction if their underlying emotion is self-contempt or self-hate.

But the interpersonal is a web, a network of interactions. We are all cause and we are all effect, influenced by and affecting all others in an endless interplay. This complex network is enormously nuanced both in time and space, duration and depth. Only those who are able to see these interactions can see the importance of wills and therefore see the possibilities to act and not least of all to change.

Insight in the web oneself inhabits, the reactions of others to oneself, one's own reactions and not least intentions, is what change life from a destructive pattern into a positive one. Nevertheless, one can never truly feel on safe ground in the sense that nothing else can go wrong. There is always a possibility that a good life can become a circle that requires much effort to get out of.

If one strives to understand interactions, one may more easily gain a clear view of constructive behaviors, and develop hope and optimism, and begin to trust oneself. One becomes aware of the fact that not only *have* one existed, and not only exist the others, but one *is and shall be*, and one is as much as others.

Not least of all, one will discover the will as its own dimension in one's life, experience the power in saying *I will*. In one's own will there exists the power not to be swept along with the currents, being controlled by coincidence and bad habits. The force of our will can help develop a new course in life.

Only the one who truly make use of his/her own will can have both a hope for the future and take responsibility for one's own life. If one has dethroned the will and surrendered life to chance, one cannot take responsibility for oneself or others. When one chooses to be a leaf in the wind, one has to avoid situations where there is too much wind. One cannot complain about being swept away. In order to survive, people with a weak or nonexistent will must seek a place where there is stagnation and a complete absence of drama and engagement.

Neither mass man nor the individual can discover the law of interaction. Mass man, because he has not developed any will, but desires to be effects of others, and be filled by them. The individual because he/she lives in a fractured arena, unable to see him/herself as anything but the cause, the dominant will. Only the person is able to see the complicated network of the reasons that bind people together, determine actions and the course of life, while also seeing how the will can break through the space between what has already happened and what can happen.

Some words on the Transcendent

As previously mentioned, social life can easily become a threat to the personal. But it is also a necessary road to the personal, there is no other. Only through intense effort to communicate and express the self in relationship to others can the person be developed. No one becomes a person in isolation.

There are also countless signs and phenomena in the interpersonal space that tell us that the week day is not merely a weekday and that mass man and individual are only phases; that also the person exists.

In many ways, daily life is based on faith, on all the transcendent phenomena that persons and the personal bring with them. It is not easy to distinguish sharply between the everyday and the festive, between the earthly and the divine. There are fleeting borders, like how sky and sea merge into one. It is also partly because of the many examples of transcendent actions or gestures in daily life that point to some reality other than the trivial and customary, both good and bad.

We experience this transcendence when we feel the need to thank someone for having received something extremely valuable, or for praying to some power to help us in our need. Or, as described in the book *A Rumor of Angels*, when we experience something terrible and inhumane, we scream to the heavens to invoke hell.[31]

American psychologist *Abraham Maslow* writes: "The important lesson gained from the true mystics is that the holy is in the normal, is present in one's daily life, in one's neighbors, friends and families, in one's backyard. . ."[32]

The mystical or transcendent can also be retrieved in the person. The person is in principle inscrutable and foreign. There are not only new possibilities in the person, but endless possibilities. We can only suspect something of that which lives in us, and in those we live with. As *Carl Gustav Jung* says, "Even the human being we think we know best, and who affirm that we do understand that him/she completely, are in some way *strangers*. He/

she is *different*. The utmost and best we can do is to assume this 'difference,' be aware of it and guard ourselves from that enormous stupidity of wanting to interpret it."[33]

That we often are unable to see the transcendent in ourselves or others may be because we take the conventional, the customary, for granted, forgetting that this is only one interpretation. We confuse reality and the understanding of it. This is also because of prejudices and the need for an answer book. We have a need for normalcy and think that life means to judge, finally "explain," and "understand." Therefore, we become blind to the inscrutable that exits in every interpersonal situation, in others and in ourselves.

The inner and interpersonal realities are necessarily both inscrutable and ambiguous. They cannot be nullified. The interpersonal is "promising," full of promises, but foreign in its nature.

We can try to standardize each other and the world through our unambiguous interpretations. Perhaps we can even further master others. We can easily fool ourselves into believing that we are in control and understand all that is worth understanding. But again and again we experience our own *shaking difference*. We will experience this in emotions we would rather not admit, in unexpected reactions, in dreams, in shameful and humiliating needs, in thoughts that suddenly appear to us as unknown, dangerous, and incomprehensible. But also in reactions that run the other way, our own goodness and selflessness can just as easily surprise us and disturb the pictures of ourselves as normal and nothing special, neither good nor evil.

Therefore we are, if we want to really understand ourselves in a greater context always *on the way*. We are on the way towards ourselves, towards knowledge about ourselves, and to the 'other' and the others. We are on a journey, always moving toward a goal that moves itself, often falls back and gains new contours. This is the transcendent, the personal; the living reality.

This is not because we like Sisyphus, continually have to roll the stone up the mountain just to see it roll back down again. But this experience, because it is not fully understood, is what makes us shape such a negative and frightening picture of human life.

Precisely, the unknown awakens fear in many. They do not dare start out on a journey without knowing where it ends, so they end up living as little as possible, living in safety and security each step of the way. Again, and again they need to assure themselves that everything is as it always has been and can never be thought to be otherwise. They are also disappointed in life itself; if it does not promise something specific, it becomes uninteresting. It is like the relationship between children and Christmas: if they are not sure they will get wonderful presents, they do not look forward to Christmas.

The experience of always being in transit, towards the transcendent, something new, means that life is alive. It is life that creates the inscrutable and ambiguous, life that makes us feel that we will never arrive. For life is an expression of an eternally creative process.

To live is therefore not about fulfilling a known form. Each living person is subject to a development that he/she does not understand and never will come to understand. The task of human beings is to let live, both in everything around them and in what is internal.

As a result, the interpersonal is always transcendent. It is transcendental due to events that are strong and demanding and because that is its nature. It is always pointing beyond itself, what one traditionally interprets it as being and it always points towards what we can never truly know.

It is at any rate unnecessary to understand it as a trip without a destination. But the destination is unknown, but that unknown destination means everything to us, keeps us alive, and makes our lives meaningful. So, we might as well travel with hope and optimism rather than depression and pessimism.

This unknown destination can fill life with joy and meaning. Because it is inscrutable and transcendent, daily life gains background and contour, becomes exciting. Personality becomes a living power, something that lies beyond one. And what is most exciting is not whether we are counted as someone by others, but whether we are able to express ourselves so that it will be understood that we know that we are, and that we will be, participants in an external as well as an internal process. Then we open up to the personal and the interpersonal; our understanding of ourselves as a person also enables others to assert their own personality.

Chapter V

Personal Reality

WE ARE INCLINED TO say that people live in different realities. What is real for one is not so for another. There are seemingly millions, even billions, of realities for us to consider, and so we must. However, in my opinion, each personal reality has certain characteristic features that recur from person to person. This is related to the fact that the personal has its own form. Personal reality teaches us that the inner and the interpersonal reality merge.

The road to reality always runs through the human being, and the subjective and the objective are inextricably interwoven one with the other. The thought of a reality independent of the mind is impossible.

To experience the structure and pattern of the personal reality, the personal must be accepted as its own dimension in our existence. The personal forces its way in, is the appearance of the self, or affirmation. The personal declares itself, offers itself irrevocably, and is something real.

The Significance of the Personal

In general, we suppose that fundamental concepts as time and space organize our experiences. We assume that our cognition, thought and language, science, and culture are determined by categories as quantity, quality, connection, and modality. Everything should be possible to experience by amount, species, condition, and type relations. In modern science, these categories are considered sufficient, and some would argue that quantities and connections are sufficient to describe reality. Some modern logicians even assert that a logical-mathematical system alone can accomplish this.

In other words, the person is viewed as standing outside of science, is at best necessary for anthropological and psychological research.

But the personal dimension is just as fundamental as these categories of natural science. The one who has experienced, thought, described and researched is crucial. Discovering the personal variable is also possible in the most exact of sciences.[34]

The personal dimension is often misunderstood to the point that some individuals are especially subjective or emotional, in contrast to more objective and rational individuals. The personal is used as an accusation and a reproach, something that one ought not to be.

But all people are unable to experience reality in any other way than their own. And naturally, since the personal is an intricate and profound interaction with the inner, interpersonal and external plane, a human being can easily misinterpret some of his/her many different symbols, feelings, thoughts, norms, values, and data that contribute to form a picture of the whole.

The question about which reality is real, yours or mine, or some of the billions of other, is meaningless. There *must* always be a consciousness related to that question. You have come full circle. The answer is therefore that for each and every one of us: *Our own reality is the real one.*

The important question is neither not about who won the competition between the different personal realities, but rather: Have we thought, felt and been attentive, so that *we know our own reality well enough*? Accusations about distortions and misrepresentations can only be directed towards people who do not know themselves, do not respect the personal and therefore are easily mistaken about their personal reality.

Our personality is our sign of distinction and nobility. Only when we are fully aware of this dimension can we see reality as something living. Then we can see that the person means something; often everything, and that we and everyone we know are significant, have effects and set their own mark on everything they experience and express, whether consciously or unconsciously.

Mind, temperament, wisdom, self-sufficiency, and purpose have an enormous effect on what *can* happen. This also suggests the boundaries of possibilities. Persons establish boundaries for what can be accomplished. The value of the person for interpersonal space is so fundamental that persons have to be counted as part of what is objectively given.

Developing understanding of the personal is comparable to developing one's judgement in the artistic arenas. There is something we must listen to intensely, with sensitivity and devotion and then let grow inside.

While one develops one's own understanding, a new reality will emerge, a reality where you can choose, act, and desire, and where engagement has value and where the creative is possible. Viewing the personal as something negative is the same as thinking that the individual should not be engaged in anything, has its own will or act.

In Plato's allegory of the cave, this personal reality is metaphorically described. Seeing the personal is like double vision, both see our existence in the shadows and are absorb with shadows, and see the light of day itself, the sun and real people.

Many may be blind to the personal exactly because it is omnipresent. It forms our lives down to the smallest details and the most vitally important choices. It is like wind and weather; an inevitable part of everything that simply happens. When something is so entirely taken for granted, it can be easy to view it as either unnecessary or a waste of time to relate to or even to think about. But to fail to see it, or concentrate on it, and listen to it, is the same as not bothering to care whether the floor and roads are full of holes you can fall through, and suddenly find yourself in the deepest dark, completely alone.

The personal is our most fundamental and most important experience and is itself the experience of what it means to be human, to be alive as a human being. Without this experience, no one could use of their possibilities, they would become empty shells, like mass man or its antithesis: the individual.

The Shape of the Personal

The personal presents a definite form. This form has a fixed rhythm: Only 'I say' is logically incomplete. To complete it we must formulate it as follows: 'I say to you; and I am awaiting your response.' Thus, the problem of the form of the personal emerges as the problem of the form of communication."[35]

The personal always implies relationships, dialogue, and communication. The person both expresses him/herself and waits for the other's expression, makes the first move or draws back, waits and is willing to participate again. While the person waits, he or she listens both to the other and to him/herself.

Seen from the outside, the person's form becomes: "an alternation of self-affirmation, and self-denial. This fundamental rhythm can be discerned in all its manifestations."[36] But seen from the inside, it becomes reciprocity between partners in a dialog either with the others, the self, or both.

Communication becomes far more than an exchange of information or a conversation. It implies an exchange of at least four perspectives or experiences. First we have the two partners as they understand themselves and next how each is understood by the other. In a dialog with another the person will have four "somebodies" to keep track of and relate to: what is expressed by the other, as wells as the other's inner reality, his/her own verbal expression, and own inner reality. This scenario can be further complicated if any psychological theories are added that include a concept of a division of the human being into three: f. example in the superego, ego and the unconscious.[37]

It is therefore unavoidable that communication becomes rather difficult. It becomes a constant speech that goes both outward and inwards simultaneously and is expressed on many levels.

The form of the personal is therefore the *coincidence, the meeting*. There are two people who relate to, confront, and stand face to face with each other, themselves, and the reality around them. Together they shape the "We" with no cost to the "I" or the "You" but in the same act. This encounter constitutes the 'I', the 'You', and the 'We', none of whom will exist outside the encounter itself.

This meeting can also be an inner meeting. When a human being meets him/herself face to face, he/she becomes a person, see the reality of the "you" and rise of the "we" as real possibilities. The space for another emerges in oneself and becomes a relation and not a limited thing.

If the form of the person is the dialogue, then the form of mass man is the conversation, and that of the individual is a monologue. While mass man never offers anything personal or anything that could deviate from the norm, the individual will provide unlimited long narratives about themselves or argue for causes. He/she often speaks both while inhaling and exhaling, and does not offer a space or an opening for contributions from anyone else. When others are speaking, the individual is thinking only of his/her next contribution.

Therefore, the form of the personal can be seen as a constant conversation, between equal and respected partners. The person becomes the conversation itself, can almost be viewed as a special language. The form of the personal is the life-breath of the interpersonal itself, breathing in and out, in and out, indefinitely. We experience, this when we answer truthfully and honestly to what another says or does, and they answer us, when we accompany each other, as if we were part of an orchestra playing the same piece of music.

The Experience of the Personal

Living in a personal reality, in the form of the personal mode, means to make some typical experiences. These can best be described as we move forward. We can interpret them as guidelines for how we have to behave if we want to live in the personal reality. They can also be viewed as directives we need to follow in order to preserve and protect our experience of the personal.

A. The most typical experience of the personal is the fundamental reality of *experience*. Regardless of our lives, our choices, or our actions, reality is experience. Everything can be traced back to experience, deep or superficial, long term or short term. That self-lived reality is *our* reality. To be real and to experience is one and the same.

This is not as trivial as it may seem. Again, it emphasizes our own value, it is we who experience, and these experiences are the frame for our lives. Therefore it is vital that we know who we are, and how we understand and relate to experience.

This experienced reality makes the subjective: people's intentions, wishes, dreams, emotions, ideas and thoughts, intentions and opinions, the foundation for all choices, both on the private and public level. Some will believe that this means we can no longer speak of an objective reality. But that is not the case. It simply means that the subjective can be understood as reality. Somewhat paradoxically, it means that in order to relate objectively to what is experienced, one must recognize the subjective reality. The person, the living subject, the perceiving consciousness, is understood first objectively if its distinctiveness is accepted.

We must make up one's mind about the experienced reality, based on the self. There is only one eyewitness, namely the self, the person. We are own eyewitnesses, our own judges, our own executioners or saviors. And we are completely reliable in the sense that nothing more reliable exists. We may make some huge mistakes about our personal reality, but we alone are supreme.

This experienced reality, is also like a thorn in our side. No matter what we do, what situation we are in, our experiences and what we do with them, play a huge roll for our fate, the fate of others, and the fate of relationships.

This is the first requirement; we need to take the distinctiveness of the subjective seriously, respect it and not try to transform it into something that it isn't, an object. The demand is to take experiences seriously, try to understand them, what they imply and can result in, what they do to the self and to others.

B. From this there come another insight, namely that the personal reality is *inhabited*, it houses us, and it is our home. The personal reality is the way it is, by necessity. Should that sound compelling and fateful, it also means that we belong absolutely to one place. We feel at home inside of our experiences, without doubt. Living in a personal reality is therefore to dwell, belong, have roots, a seat in the universe that is ours alone and can only be filled only by us.

The moment that we abandon the personal or do not find it, cannot answer it, the world becomes uninhabitable and we become homeless, without an anchor anywhere, we experience nothing that makes an impression on us. In the absence of the personal, madness threatens.

That the personal is habitable suggests the next demand: we must acknowledge our experiences and *make* our world habitable, make it livable for both ourselves and for others. We cannot keep the house shut, for it would then become uninhabitable for us too. Neither can we let just anyone in. But we must let in those with whom we can share a personal company.

C. A third structure within the personal reality is where existence can come to us as an entirety. We experience it as a *totality*, and we ourselves are a whole. We are not a *tabula rasa*,[38] empty and featureless, and the world around us is not divided, empty, or insignificant.

In the beginning, the world came to us entire and complete. As children we experienced the world as a whole—which of course does not mean that we experienced the whole world. But the world was connected from morning to night, our most diverse tasks blended together; the day was a process and not divided up into thousands of unrelated tasks. Perhaps it is true that the child's world is small, but it is also very near and overwhelmingly *present*. Later we learned that the world was too big for us, and that it was split into thousands of atoms.

In the experience of the personal, that wholeness returns to our lives. It fills us and we fill it. When we love, we clearly discover this experience. The beloved is complete, we are ourselves complete when together with the beloved—to love is to gather together in one feeling the self and the other, meeting in a complete encounter.

From this comes the norm to work for completion. The more we can gather together what has been scattered, the more we manage to create connections, draw lines between the most unexpected, the more we will be able to promote the personal in each situation. The more we can discern the lines of communication in ourselves, recognize all of our phases, in each other, see the patterns in our interests and values, the more whole we will be for ourselves.

In daily life, this requires concentration and few tasks. We must make sure that we have continuous time and possibilities to delve deeply into what we are doing, take things one at a time. Not least of all, we have to arrange for silence, external conditions that allow us space for reflection and experiences of wholeness. In our extremely troubled, taxing and noisy times, this is something we need to plan for in order to succeed. We have to *want* peace and quiet, *want* interaction and wholeness, and ourselves arrange our daily life to be filled with a minimum of these.

D. In the experience of personal reality, we will moreover declare that it is *ours*, it belongs to us together. Through the personal, we pay attention to the fact that we are together, that we are never alone, that we live in a plurality that is impossible to ignore.

The impression of being alone in the world, arise from mixing uniqueness with loneliness. Each has his/her own perspective and personality, but what we illuminate is what we have in common, just like how a red and blue spotlight can illuminate the same landscape. We also have in common the peculiar *that* we light up and do so in our own special way. By this it can be said that we transcend the loneliness that is created by the fact that we light up in very different ways.

Personal reality is not a landscape that no others can enter. Being a person is about receiving and sharing. In being together, the person is always available and decentralized, which means that others are always incorporated into the person's reality. Therefore, it is inescapable that we share the world with others. How much or how little and how will vary from person to person, but *that* we share will not change.

From this we can draw the rule about sharing, laying our reality open, ensuring that we ourselves are as reciprocal as possible. Naturally without compromising when our personality is concerned. We shall not be obliterated by fellowship like mass man, or as the individual try to stand above it, but rather assert our uniqueness *and* strive for cooperation. It is only as a person that we have a common reality, not as an individual. The individual will always be isolated in its own world, while the mass man/woman never takes a look into he/her separate reality, but shares with others even the 'personality' he/she doesn't has.

E. Experiencing the presence of the fellowship means that we can catch sight of a fifth structure. The personal reality belongs to us, it is our own *possession*, is not empty or distant, but here and now and, not least of all, it is ours.

This ownership evokes many possible power struggles and creates hierarchies. There are many who would happily assume control over our property and try to convince us that they own our personal reality. Parents will try to make us believe that they know better than we what we feel and think, make us believe that we are simply an extension of their inner and outer reality. Teachers will try to turn us into obedient pupils and other societal authority figures will unfailingly try to make us one of their supporters. Spouses, sweethearts, and friends will often imagine that they can decide and control us. We ourselves will often be tempted to do the same to others.

This battle involves the personal reality of each and every human being. Some will quickly choose to surrender and let someone else take over. But abdication inevitably causes powerlessness that leads to sickness, whether physical or psychological. Should one attempt to let someone own one, one will always end up a wreck. Allowing oneself to be owned is a devaluation of the self, and there is no property of any value left behind.

To want to own someone else is a devaluation of them, to suppose they are objects without owners. It is also to assume, that oneself is the master not a person. Only individuals can own others, persons can only engage themselves in and for others. To own someone has much less value than being friends.

In the interpersonal reality the battle around property rights is much more intense than it is in the world of things.

This determines a new norm: we have to fight for the ownership rights to our own personal reality. We can't just be the legal owners but also the real power brokers.

That means that we must constantly work to ensure that our feelings, thoughts, choices and actions are really *ours*. We have to find what we are behind all the conventions, and all that ostensibly makes us who we are. "As I find myself behind things, and that as mind, so I must later find *myself* also behind *thoughts*, to wit as their creator and *owner*. . . If I destroy their (the thoughts) corporeity, I take them into mine, and say: 'I alone am corporeal.' And now I take the world as it is to me, as *mine*; I refer all to myself . . . as owner I thurst spirits or ideas into their "vanity." They have no longer any power over me, as no "earthly might" has power over the spirit."[39]

We must oppose any attempts to take over/abandon the personal property rights to our own existence. A human being is obligated to fight for the right to self and to expect that others will do likewise. Therefore, the norm implies the *duty* to both liberate oneself and to set others free. The one who desire to become an adult has to claim full ownership of oneself, and never accept to own the others no matter how much they may ask for it. Parents have the duty to let their children go even if the children ask for something else.

That we are always the owners of our own selves forces us to be real. We have to throw out our occupiers and remove those who besiege us. We can accomplish this through expanding our consciousness about what is real, true, good and beautiful for us. This is a solitary battle and must be waged by each human being. In principle it cannot be passed on to anyone else.

The personal reality is accordingly no comfortable secret, nor a refuge or oasis of peace and tranquility, nor an automatic sacrifice for someone else's well-being. More than anything else, personal reality is like a battle zone, a point for the thousands of different lights on the world.

Now and then, these norms can naturally come into conflict should you try to apply them mechanically. Some may believe that sharing their reality with others is at odds with owning the self completely and wholly. But that is not true. The wealthy can safely share or let others borrow its goods while the poor have nothing to either give or lend. Only the one who is indisputably in complete charge of self can share ones reality with others. The ones who let him or herself be governed by the authorities, have nothing left that grow out of the riches off the personality. No matter how "service-minded" this individual may seem, pettiness will be the most noticeable.

The Choice

To become owners of our particular personal reality force us to accept the fundamental reality of our choice.

Previously, we have perhaps only been aware of our choices when a crisis looms or when we have clearly and distinctly been confronted with more than one possibility. When we for example have to choose, related to education, career, sickness and divorce or other urgent problems.

Many will claim that they themselves have never experienced a choice or had a choice. They have done precisely what is expected of them, followed the path that their parents, their environment or fate had placed in front of them. When in old days, one spoke of genes, today one speaks of environment. Both are now considered equally fateful.

Some will claim that only people with "resources" can choose, and that choice is dependent on wealth, class, talent, and prosperity. A common man/woman, from the middle or working class is not supposed to have choices. They have to take what they can get. They act under duress. But the choice, that is relevant here, is not a choice about being rich or happy, to have all wishes fulfilled, or to accomplish fantastic feats.

This existential choice revolves around expressing the self *or* expressing others, to act from the self *or* from others. This is a choice about reality, authenticity, honesty, openness and morality, a choice of position. The question becomes whether one is one's own spokesman or a bystander or DAS MAN.[40] Do one express what one really experience? Is one honest and authentic? Or are one disguised, representative, conventional, and role-determined? One has to choose between two worlds.

In our consumer society everybody is apparently able to make a choice. Choice is incorporated into daily life. In stores we choose from countless types of goods, in our spare time among many types of entertainment offerings, friends, and possibilities. Choosing is something we are trained to do from childhood.

Perhaps this is why we imagine that choice is always visible, external, exterior, and costs money. Or because choice is accompanied by crises, we think choosing is dangerous.

But the existential choice does not necessarily imply crisis or that something is easily grasped. Choosing personal reality is a choice between our own laws and insights and the ones that we think belong to others or the universal. Often it is a choice between an unknown terrain that is close at hand and a known but distant terrain, which we can call manners. Or it is between us and a stronger/weaker and more or less strange individual. It becomes a choice between long-term living processes and short term, stiff, well established routines.

Moreover, it is a perpetual choice. Again, and again we will be thrown into this choice. It is inescapable. Should we show who we are, or should we keep it hidden, pretend there is nothing wrong, go along and maybe even manage to fool the others—and possibly ourselves? Should others get a false picture of us? During all those times we don't have clarity in ourselves, in our thoughts, feelings, positions and values, should we still open up and reveal our insecurity, doubt, confusion, and vulnerability? This can often be a question of winning power or losing face.

That is why this choice is deeply ethical, a choice between honesty and insincerity, growth and defeat, development and stagnation.

Choosing to be oneself is not just about choosing honesty. It is also about choosing something that has a fruitful effect on our relationships to other people; one chooses development within interpersonal relationships. Now and then honesty can have a negative effect, something that happens if the other is scared to death to be well off, happy, and honest. In such cases, we are faced with neurotic or other psychically damaged individuals. A deeper understanding of human nature force its way in when we embrace our choice.

The existential choice is also to choose fear and dizziness as *Kierkegaard* says, fear is the dizziness of freedom.[41] It is only in moments now and then we will be completely clear to ourselves, often tainted by the confusion around us and inside us. "One has to search oneself to find, amongst the litter of distracting motives, so much as a desire to seek this living unity, then to listen patiently for what it may whisper to one, to test it in struggle and obscurity, and even then one can never be sure that one grasps its meaning. It resembles, more than anything, a secret voice, calling to us to in a language that we would have to spend our lives learning; which is why the word 'vocation' describes it better than any other."[42]

And of course, for the most part, we don't have a choice. As long as we are alive, the personal reality, and ourselves as persons, will be present as an enormous power, a power that will repeatedly break through our views and in into our hiding places. The person will always exist in shadows of roles we inhabit and the impersonal, and always throw a cast on all that we experience.

Therefore, choice is also fate. To refrain from choosing oneself is like fleeing from your own fate; it is the same thing as not wanting to be who you always are anyway. To flee from fate without being overtaken by it sooner or later, in some sense or other, is not a possibility.

As a result, the ability to choose is the deepest content and reality of human life. To live is to experience the doubts of your own choices and to express a multifaceted, malleable and agile material: yourself.

We also constantly choose what relates to the ambiguous, the unknown, that part of ourselves and others that we can never quite capture with our theories, ideologies, concepts or signs. Periodically, the enigma washes over everything and everyone, the inscrutable can seem like the most dominant presence in our existence. It can seem impossible to understand anything at all. To know becomes knowing that one knows nothing.[43]

In our human existence there is an even more complicating factor, namely the constantly contradictory dimensions to which we are connected. Are we animals or divine creatures? Are we immortal or mortal? To the extent we experience and believe the one or the other, experience the duplicity or not, can be decisive for our entire lives.

To choose will imply the ability to experience and interpret "both-and," and see the very different possibilities and tasks. Choosing is easy if part of the diversity is defined away. Each situation is unique, and each relationship is completely special. We must, as persons, choose the human whole, which means always expressing this "both—and," choose both life and death in a bearable balance. "In our fear of death, we experience the 'gravity of the negative', and it is therefore a necessary clue that enables us to determine what is essential and what is not essential.[44]

To relate to values and worlds that one experience as contrary to and complementary to what one really stand for, is therefore decisive for the substance and the consequence of one's choice. If the large parts of lived life, perhaps especially the dark and frightening parts, are kept away from both reflection and emotion, then choices of course will only occur on the surface. The honesty one believes one is expressing is false; one is simply mistaken about oneself, even if the intention was the best. In order to be oneself one must also live oneself, to choose oneself implies the courage to live in reality.

Like the person, these daily choices must therefore be like a dialogue, formulated so that they confirm, not just polarity, but the context itself, and in this way express a series of polarities. We must see to during the course of our lives that we always choose *moment and duration, similarity and difference, satisfaction and dissatisfaction, stimulation and stabilization, proximity and distance,* in a harmonious and fruitful mixture.[45] Should we fall too far onto one side of these polarities, our quality of life will suffer, and we will experience being half and emptiness.

The choice must be a distinct part of our lives. Life must be planned and lived so that we always find ourselves in the middle of the choice, always able to choose, and not stuck in a pattern. Such a pattern can be that which only gives the moment, conformity, satisfaction, stimulation and closeness, something many women will have a tendency to choose. Another will only give permanence, difference, self-denial, stability and distance, which is perhaps the usual choice of men.

Mass man/woman has the inclination to choose "the feminine side" of the polarity. He/she will go with the flow of the moment, have fun, satisfy their needs at all times, constantly want to be entertained and stimulated, and preferably be the audience in the front row seats at all the main events. Modern sexual morality is for example typical for the mass man, he/she is stimulated by sex films and pornography, give in to their sexual desires independent of the personal, have sex with as many as possible, but take minimal responsibility.

The individual will choose "the macho side" and dream about immortal deeds and monuments, forsake a great deal in order to perfect oneself, and keep vibrant, daily reality at a distance. Old-fashioned monogamous sexual morals suit the individual, and result in few needs, little appetite, inhibition, while taking on a great deal of responsibility and many duties. The individual has learned to steel him/herself since the goal belongs to a different stratosphere.

Double standards in morality can often be an expression for the division between the two phases. In order to see this, it is important to remember that double standards also changes with the particular fashions of the times.

If we shall be able to live as persons we therefore have to choose the *choice* itself. We must recognize that the choice must always be a reality, and work to express both the self and the personal structure of human reality. To choose that alternative means that we choose the personal as basis for the existence. Only the personal contains the inscrutable and unknown, the complex and the ambiguous, the many polarities—and the choice itself.

Chapter VI

Personalizing Processes

It is usually easy for people to abstain from the personal. The vast majority of situations will not encourage it. For this reason, many will doubt themselves as a person and will be confused about how to express oneself more clearly.

As previously mentioned, it is difficult to convey the experience of the personal. One reason is that everyone has his or her own unique experiences, so it often becomes a question of interpretation. Furthermore, it is only after people have actually experienced themselves as persons that they find meaning in words that describe the personal. This distinctive dimension requires experience in order to be understood and conveyed just as the dimension of color requires that one can see. Explaining color to the blind or music to the deaf is a next to impossible task.

Sometimes the situation isn't always so difficult. Most of us, as mentioned earlier, have experiences of this sort to look back on. We have to dig deep and develop these experiences more fully; redesign them as an inspiration and a reality. Once again, I want to stress just how important it is to *want* the personal; only then can we catch sight of the complete human being and its innate possibilities.

In this chapter I will suggest some different ways to move forward when one wants to personalize your world as much as possible.

Looking for the real

Everyone realizes that they can make mistakes about their own experiences, emotions, and thoughts. Now and then errors in judgment are so great that the issue is actually about what is and what is not real. Hallucinations, illusions, and misconceptions are most common phenomena.

The work to personalize one's own world begins here. We have to try to understand what truly lives inside us, what or whom is truly real to us. It is temporary where one begins. Increasing insight into one's own reality will lead to increasing insight into the reality of others. Finding the way to what is real requires a great deal of effort and the will to avoid being fooled.

It can be easier to start with others. We can often instinctively feel how others play a role or have a position that doesn't suit them or is something alien to them, and does not come from within. We hear false tones somewhere, and we notice tension and anxiety as they seem to circle around themselves and their own, and are incapable of dialogue, they represent something that they don't are. Then it happens, as mentioned before, that we part with others with an empty feeling and loss of meaning, we have not met anybody and have not been seen. The feeling of unreality, follow all situations where we and/or others, are not ourselves.

If we want to be able to express ourselves as persons, we have to consciously seek out people who are genuine to us, who we experience as authentic and genuine. These are the people who can give us an experience, who can engage us and let us go home with a sense of meaning. These types of friends and acquaintances will help us express our own reality as clearly as possible.

We must systematically search for the experiences that are valuable and especially real. This could be time with family, children, the elderly, animals; it could mean experiences that put us in touch with nature or physical fitness and sports, spiritual endeavors or art and cultural experiences, or work that has meaning. Whatever it is we are most concerned with, that most takes hold of us and makes us feel whole, that is what is most real for us. In this we find the source and the road to understanding ourselves as persons.

A. We meet our reality often in our *strong emotions*. Other persons, things, or affairs, that we feel strongly about, are probably real to us, whether that feeling is passionate or foolish. But our intense emotions can sometimes turn concrete persons and phenomena into symbols of what is real. We can therefore also be fooled by our own passions as they divert our attention.

B. A second path goes through our *loyalties*. Only the fewest of us can sustain cynicism and indifference and live a life without any responsibilities for ourselves or for others. After evaluating whether or not our loyalties for something or someone are adequate or whether they are simply an expression of our choices or have been forced on us, we will find what binds us to reality, what anchors us to existence. It is here that we find the core of reality that can be developed in order to elevate the feeling of a vital existence.

C. Reality expresses itself in what we deem *holy*, what we honor and respect. Cynicism is often a shell for the disillusioned human to hide behind. Everyone can search behind their disappointments and rediscover what they once held sacred.

It can be worthwhile to be systematic about the effort. We can analyze our disappointments and find the reason for the cynicism. Bad experiences with relationships that you may have caused yourself out of thoughtlessness can result in losing one's belief in love. Practicing to keep sacred all one regards as valuable, no matter how small a thing that may be, can breathe some life in the emptiness.

We can also make lists of all the things on which we're really spending our time and using our energy. These lists can inform us about our values, and we can consider whether we should prioritize things differently. Cynicism can be connected to a life spent on indifferent things.

If we agree on the things that with certainty are real for us, we can look at ourselves from the outside and know what we should work with and who we should be with to develop our selves. The feeling of not being able to express ourselves may be connected to the fact that we spend too little time and energy on precisely that and those who are real to us. We are simply too lazy, or do not manage our time well. Mismanagement is also a possibility for the individual. It affects both others and us.

D. Perhaps the best way to gain some insight into what is real in and outside of us may be to search for and expand upon our understanding of the *inscrutable and unique*, two sides of the same coin. In the unique we always catch a glimpse of the inscrutable. At the very moment we experience something or someone inscrutable, when we just can't find the words to describe the thing or the other, we also experience the unique. For example, when we are in love, the beloved is both unique and inscrutable. When the inscrutable disappears, the unique will disappear with it.

E. In general, what is *real* to us is what we find *meaningful*. Wherever we can find even the slightest bit of meaning, some tenuous feeling of significance, we will find what is real both in ourselves and/or in others. Then we will find the road we must follow.

If someone for example finds meaning, in drugs and alcohol, and experiences this as a genuine, even proper life, it may be because these poisons offer highly coveted experiences. People are awake and feel happiness, love, aggression, and strong feelings that make minutes and hours, worth living. The problem is that it is not real. But the experience can become a path to the reality of one individual. What provides value in the alcohol, it may also find elsewhere. Alcoholics need insight into what other than alcohol that can give the same lively feeling of existence.[46]

Reality in us and in our surroundings will reverberate, respond, echo; sooner or later we will bump into it. It is solid, hard, sharp-edged, but also soft and warm, meaningful and fruitful.

And not least of all, others will notice this. When we are ourselves, we are creative in our time together, we relate to others. It can mean love or confrontation, but it will always be engagement.

We are seismographs; we pay attention to reality when we approach and when we depart. Emptiness, joy, or sorrow tells us how far away we are. Life and the glow in our own eyes show if we are accessible, if the other can meet us.

To become real is to find one's engagements, one's loyalties, what is sacred, one's inscrutability and uniqueness, what gives one meaning: becoming a person and personalizing one's own existence. The methods and the motives for doing this can be many, but if one is able to find something to hold on to, the result is the same. Reality comes through.

Looking for the Good

One of the major roads to the personal runs through ethical growth. Expressing the personal is like endeavoring to lead a good life. Therefore, our ethics can be a measure of how personal we intend and manage to be.

Lack of meaning and sense of unreality can be caused by avoidance of moral actions and opinions, or that one clearly acts in such a way that oneself knows is immoral or cowardly.

Cowardice is something of particular concern. If one fails to act in a situation, when one is convinced that somebody should act or to state an opinion, there will be repercussions. One may feel shame, feel small and conquered by others, and feel as nobody. Even insignificant cowardice will remove a piece of our personality and elicit unreality. Each time, one does not show who one is, one will not oneself feel that one is. Emptiness will slowly seep in.

In this sense, it is important to be aware that *weakness* is often another word for cowardice. A so-called weak human being, is also someone who never shows who he/she really is, always waiting for others to do the right thing or say what should be said. The weak will lose more and more of the feeling of being; it is always others who are someone. The loss of feeling of being, arise from lack of distinctness in company of others. The feeling of not being someone correctly describes the place for the weak. We feel like someone not at least when we are brave, able to show courage. If we don't expect anything from the weak, always making excuses for the one concerned, often means the same as saying he/ she should just go on being nobody.

Strength and courage correspond to but do not coincide with social status. Some people are perhaps more willing to express themselves when they feel that they are somebody in others eyes. This does not need to mean that they are brave. Courage is an internal characteristic and is best developed in situations where one's authority and place in a given hierarchy is not taken for granted, but is risked.

Immorality will always take a little bit of self away from the one concerned. It then becomes necessary to erect a façade and ensure its preservation and construction. The face presented to the outside world becomes more important than self-respect. Living in a state of more or less immoral will mean a slow dissolution of the personality. Left behind is only the façade. The roles played in life can therefore be understood as lies, similar to a bad actor learning to master a role without really managing to live inside the character for even one second. The actor becomes an actor playing an actor.

The road to personal reality runs through simple daily courage. One speak up about ones views, act when there is need to create justice and goodness. One dares to confront, here and now. Courage is best developed in close relationships, stopping children from throwing stones at cats and birds, adults from being violent towards children, and attempting to be universally nice and helpful. Such moral actions everyone should have sufficient fantasy to imagine and enough experience to know that in these areas one most often don't act.

Perhaps most importantly, a human being, that consciously work for what is the good, will also dare to experience evil, and be able to see one's own *guilt*. Courage implies also the ability to feel guilt and shame. The weak or the cowardly do not have the strength to carry one's own guilt. Modern man acts as if guilt no longer exists; therefore they often have no sense of shame in their lives.

Guilt and *shame* are essential aspects of self-knowledge, not because one should cry about one's own vileness and develop a negative form of self-centeredness, but to understand in depth one's responsibility for one's own existence. To experience guilt and shame is necessary to limit oneself in relation to others, and see what concerns only one self. Guilt and shame create boundaries and give people contours and guidelines. They are also useful reminders about humility; to be good comes not easily to arrogant people, they do not have the will to be responsible. While responsibility tells something about future actions, guilt tells something about the past and the will to make things right and to do penance. Acting for the good is not just about the future, it's also about being able to make things right again.

Moral actions make one visible both to the self and others. Such actions enable one to say 'I' and to feel real, experience that others are real, that they are the 'YOU'. One may feel sorry for the moral weak and want to help and protect them, but one cannot feel the personal existence in them. They seem empty, even to those who don't demand anything from them, they can't be experienced by anyone.

The road to the self also then runs through ethical strength and goodness. By taking action that is ethically good, one becomes a character, a clear contour; becomes SOMEBODY, and this somebody is not a lie, construction or pretense.

A moral human being will develop a specific mind being, showing tolerance, because one understands one's own diversity, can live and let live.[47]

When one finds the good, one no longer sees the world through negatives, but through positives, awakened, full of color, sounds, acts and persons.

Looking for the Truth

Another key road, focus on truth.

Lies and *dishonesty* blur and demoralize the person. It can be difficult to determine just where to draw the line, like for so-called white lies, lies uttered to protect others. One way to determine is to evaluate what feelings in others one is considering when one is lying to them for the best. Is it vanity or the others feeling of status? Or is it anxiety and uncertainty? The latter can give meaning, while the former do not. One may also evaluate whether it is oneself one is trying to protect against the strong feelings of others, their anger or aggression. Are white lies a shield one can hide behind? If so, the white lie can be an expression of cowardice and become destructive. If the lie protects because there is real danger around, that is a different matter.

But dishonesty is also often expressed indirectly. It may take on the characteristics of bluff or unreliability. The topic one has an opinion about, one really doesn't know anything about. The one who is bluffing will accumulate anxiety and uncertainty, experience one's own falsehood, and live in fear of being exposed.

Therefore, *love of truth* has many dimensions. One of these is the search for truth itself, an inexhaustible impatience and longing. The other is the will to express what one know or believe to be true in any context, if not some superior reason, like the protection of a human life, speak against.

To develop as a person assumes both processes, both a persistent search and the highest degree of clarity.

The truth must also be sought outside of words. In action, manner, expression, clothing, and outer things, one must truthfully try to express who one is and how one understands the world. If one doesn't do that, one's personality can be dominated by affectation and pretense. This is often hard to judge. This may be difficult to determine. The boundary between being fashionable and being pretentious and snobby is fluid. Again, the criterion may be feelings. Is one dressing in a particular way because one wants to resemble others, impress, or play a role or because one is actually expressing something real in oneself?

When one struggles to find the truth and express it, will there be consequences to the consciousness. To work with the truth will expand the consciousness; one will be able to understand and acknowledge more, see more, and the mind will illuminate new areas and standards. The mind becomes both more comprehensive and profound. Increasing awareness is impossible unless it occurs in the company of truth and reality—all other form of awareness is brainwashing and empty ideology.

As part of the work to find truth, we can also strive *to put our actions into a greater connection*, and to evaluate them intellectually based on the morals we believe to be good. Ask the question, do one want others to act as oneself act?[48] If the answer is no, that the action that should be reserved for one self and one's acquaintances, one can be pretty sure that the action cannot be defended as moral. We can also ask the question about the consequences or value of actions and evaluate them out of a demand to maximize good. Or we can try to listen to the innate value of the action and answer the question in deepest possible honesty.

The most important consideration has to be whether the action will increase the qualities of the fellowship, whether it creates deeper and better personal relationships. In personalist philosophy, dialogue will be the criterion. Does the action leave space for a 'You', or is it a pure ego trip? Is it so expansive that it will make the fellowship more genuine and deeper, or is it destructive? If the latter, then we must also evaluate the action in the long term; a falling out over time can be fruitful for personal relationships.

Different theories about ethics can be used advantageously; but the main criterion is always your own honesty and insight into what is good. People who do not have their own experiences with what is good cannot determine if an action is good.

The truth must be loved as highly as goodness. The more truthful one becomes in ones thousands of different expressions, verbal or nonverbal, the more real one become. Being truthful is the same as being real. Falsehood, broadly, will conceal oneself both for oneself and for others. What one cannot show to others, one will also not see. Like goodness, being true is to be awakened into existence.

Looking for the Beautiful

Just as important as the previous roads towards a personal existence is the beautiful. Beauty gathers us, grabs us and lifts us up, heals us, and makes us whole. Everybody knows how nature, people, animals, music, philosophy, art, and literature can affect us. The beautiful is the direct experience of the unique, mystical, and holy, something to which one must yield.

Much is clearly beautiful. One doesn't have to look far to find it. To the contrary, beauty will occasionally seek one out. Despite this, a human being's condition may not allow him or her to experience the beautiful, even by the best of intentions. Music becomes noise, nature becomes pesky mosquitoes or cold wind, people stereotypes, literature and philosophy just words.

Such a condition is often connected to a conviction that nothing means anything, with cynicism and values-nihilism. And because such convictions also will devalue human beings to themselves, the personal will soon assert itself again, and the longing for beauty will become persisting, and the hunt for beauty vital.

The most important remedy is to increase *the normal sensuality* and develop the five senses: smell, taste, sight, hearing and touch. This means the same as regaining the center of gravity in the body, being aware of the role of the body for the quality of life. A body that is not used or one that has been damaged will not even pick up the most normal sensory experiences; the smoker will have the sense of smell damaged. Those who can only carry out routine experiences all day long will not notice how the meat balls taste.

A physically active lifestyle combined with meditation can train the sensory faculties both internally and externally, while adding far more and exciting impressions. Changes, the will to try something new, can sharpen the sensory perception. One doesn't necessarily need overwhelmingly strong experiences in order to understand that you are sensual.

This sensuality is as much spiritual as it is physical. The will has to be used; perception must be concentrated. You have to move into the body mentally in a new way, not halfway, unwilling and shameful, but fully and completely be present into one's own body. Then the body becomes something that one is, and not an object that sometimes fools you, and sometimes is an obstacle, and only occasionally a joy. You become your own body, because body and soul merge together.

When body and soul merge together one will experience beauty. Therefore, the nature of the soul or the psyche is also important. The soul cannot settle in the body if it is run down and abused, and the soul itself is broken or absent.

To reach spiritual wholeness, healing, implies harmonizing diversity and contradictions in the soul.

Harmony is a concept that is often misunderstood. It does not mean that one should try to standardize or create idyll; has nothing to do with lovely facades or success. Harmony is something musical, with many different notes or sounds that combine. Harmony is a general impression that emerges when something really belongs together. A human being who is simply friendly can also be dissonant if the sound is not pleasant. Harmony doesn't imply that one cannot be aggressive or angry. When appropriate, aggression and anger should be expressed, but the harmonic human being is not crude and does not lose the ability to formulate a message about what has caused his or her anger.

Harmony represents the integration of the complex and the contradictory, the acceptance of the human condition, an expression of life. One swings back and forth between contradictions without determining something as the true 'I', and without submitting what one do not tolerate to some kind of shadow existence that one is afraid of and want to fight. What is part of the human being is not seen as dangerous in itself.

Disharmony means cacophony, emptiness, dissonance in the human being, falseness, immaturity, duplicity. One becomes featureless and plays on only one or two strings. When one harmonizes one self, the unknown and the inscrutable gain a central place; all of the characteristics of the person can be expressed and live in balance.

That many in our culture are afraid of both their body and soul is a fact that prevents full sensory experiences. It is useless to tell people that there is nothing to be afraid of, because that is not so. There is a lot in the body and soul that has seductive power and the whole human being can be swept away given the opportunity to do so. Even if that is not dangerous in and of itself, there is always the possibility of danger for that one particular human being.

But the ethical and personal will act as a barrier against crises and catastrophes. One will partly be able to avoid and partly transform danger by finding wholeness where the negative has its place, like shadows in the evening have a place in the day.

A person, a whole body and soul, is a human being who knows with all senses that he/she exists, the rhythm of the blood is felt almost down to the little toe, the heart's throb and lungs breathing accompany each other. People like this literally see the surrounding world in a new light, a light other than the veiled and blurred conventional light, a light that lets them see mountains and valleys where they previously saw only flatlands.

The sensual human being expands the sensory perceptions. It is almost like hearing pictures, seeing sounds, tasting touch, and touching the invisible. All phenomena gain new dimensions. Not least of all, they gain permanence, both in the sense of time, lasting longer, and in the sense of consistency, they gain a new solidity.[49]

When in a concentration camp during the Second World War *Oscar Magnusson* had this experience: "Can a crust of bread be something other than a crust of bread? . . . There is something in the substance that no one can know anything about—and there are places in the human body that no one really knows anything about –only in our ability to concentrate our attention on the details can our ability to survive be explained. . . . We could take one pea and enjoy it with the tongue until we were completely satisfied with that one pea, until we understood its special construction. I can assure you that a pea is a miracle—readers of this book have no ideas what a pea contains."[50]

Sensuality becomes a distinct lifestyle that promotes the person and reveals human potential. The body and soul become one complete sense with many dimensions, attentive and receptive. Simultaneously, it becomes one expression, a harmonic melodious picture of the personality. The whole is more important than details in sensuality; but also details gain a significance that was previously overlooked.

Seeking the personal is also consistently to beautify one's own existence.

One can start simply; collect what is beautiful and make oneself beautiful. Ugly things, clothes, and "beauty defects" that are easily remedied should be dealt with. By their ugliness they affect our senses, which will slowly become less receptive. Living surrounded by ugly things is distressing even if one might become fond of the objects for different reasons. Sentimental value should not be disdained.

But the unaesthetic, no matter what form it takes, is disgusting. We turn away and do not want to sense. Experiencing human denigration, for example in concentration camps, forces one to shut down the senses completely. Oscar Magnusson also tells about how he developed a technique that helped him, so he no longer saw what was terrible; he had to erect a mental shield that took him a long time to shake off.[51]

If one gets too many mental shields, also the beautiful is shut out. All people, also those who through their work are forced to deal with the unaesthetic, need to create lagoons, oases of beauty.

The process of beautification ought to be far more pervasive, than it is in our culture today. Art and culture must be part of daily life, as often as possible, one should seek out nature. How to do this depends on the individual, but that it must happen is certain. TV series like "Dynasty" have their mission in this matter; it is the beauty of the people, the clothes, and the interiors that explain the popularity of the series.

Correspondingly, as mentioned earlier, if we only surround ourselves with obvious beauty, the lack of wholeness will make things seem flat. Beauty can be pure consumption; the lover of beauty, the aesthete, can't drink from an ordinary glass. To truly cultivate beauty means also to be able to see beauty where no others can see it, and perhaps even where most will swear none can exist.

Beauty challenges us to try to find it in everything. No one can live only with beauty, for the unaesthetic can also be found in us, our bodies. An exaggerated preoccupation of the obviously beautiful can conceal self-contempt and the individualistic need for immortality. Beauty is found first and foremost in evanescence.

We can learn to experience beauty; collect objects, visit beautiful places, have beautiful experiences, and meet beautiful people. Everybody can think beautiful thoughts, thoughts that make one seeing. Ugly and evil thoughts can satisfy revenge and hate, but they will unavoidably make mental blinds go down.

Surrounding ourselves with the beautiful is a lifetime project, like harmonizing one's own personality. But once one starts, one will recognize more and more of oneself as a person, and experience others that way. In one sense, one can say the person is always beautiful; the human being who is able to express him/herself will always impress us with a distinct kind of beauty. In such cases one can claim that appearances mean little.

Looking for the Horizon

When someone says that a human being lacks a horizon, it means readily that this human being lacks depth of dimension and is not conscious of the interaction in his or her life.

Lack of horizon can be a sign of immaturity. But it can also be a sign of stagnation and inner tension. When experienced as habitual and predictable, reality is thoroughly boring. All that exists are, one believes, the fixed dead things and the ordinary routines.⁵² The human being is tightly bound to daily, practical tasks, and concrete sensory experiences. Perception and reflection levels are low.

Everything that seems to express something other than what is normal is defined away. Dreams, hallucinations, and occult phenomena are viewed *only* as unreal. The openness that other cultures have for the paranormal is viewed as odd or primitive. Likewise, everything from religious experiences to natural medicine is called nonsense; one chooses *not* to relate everything outside of hard cold reality.

This oversimplification of existence is also transferred to attitudes about people and relationships between people. The human being becomes unexciting, easily understood. The world is split into two. Some choose a world without drama; they believe that if they have the best of intentions and do their best, and all will end up fine. Because they believe that they survive, so survive the world. And others choose the exact opposite reality; they believe others always act from their own petty self-interests, and that only strong egoists and individualists will survive.⁵³

But in the interpersonal as in nature, the horizon is endless and always there. The horizon is all that we don't relate to all the time, but take for granted or define away. Sooner or later, we have to turn our gaze to the horizon. The complementary, the complex, the ambiguous and its opposite vibrate in existence like the misty haze on a summer morning.

Finding oneself as a person and manage to personalize one's own existence is like working to integrate one's own special horizon, living with what is one's complement. The complementary makes our reality understandable, just as black enables us to see white and vice versa. Our horizon is the background for our choices and adds content to our actions. Thoughtlessness is actions that are not attempted illuminated by the horizon. The horizon forces us to choose anew, looms continually over our existence and gives it new dimensions. The horizon makes us come alive. Additionally, it gives daily life character and reality. Without the complementary, what one believes to be reality becomes empty and false. It means nothing and is of no concern to anyone.

In my philosophy, the horizon represents something both the very complex and something very contradictory. While mass man lives happily in a reality of absolute certainty and a completely fluid horizon, somewhat chaotic and without substance or constancy, the individual has a chaotic, contentious daily life and a sure and certain horizon. In our times, those who are considered borderline, live a daily life without boundaries between individuals and their territory. For them all the boundaries between the 'I' and the 'you', have disappeared, respect and trust are only words, the narcissistic individuals takes the law into their own hands, almost on a whim. The horizon is completely absent.

Because of this complexity I will here analyze the meaning of the horizon first and foremost in an ethical and emotional perspective.

There is nothing a human being does, that can remove evil and good from his/her own existence or from the world as such. No actions can make what is complementary disappear; it is part of people as well as outside of them.

Behind lies, evil, hate, and indifference, there exists truth, goodness, love and engagement. Because of that the opposite makes an impression and has value. Lies are lies because the truth is true, lies refer to something that does not exist, while truth refers to something that does exist and says so. In the same way, the negative makes the positive valuable, we learn at least to value love from others when we know how hate destroys us.

Simultaneously, the negative has its own reality; it is not simply a world of shadows. People do actually lie, and hate, and are evil. And this does not just happen coincidentally or accidently. It happens because it is willed, wished for, and sometimes even valued. Nazi crimes were not committed only by mad men, or uncontrolled feelings. They were the result of a planned evil; the goal was to create the new human being—a godlike being. Whether or not the Nazi's had to sacrifice millions of people were trifles to them.[54]

Even today many political movements and ideologies use hate, to gather supporters around causes and to promote liberation. Individuals too, can also be extremely thorough in their arguments about why they have the right to harm other people.

We all experience quite an intense hatred when we hear about recklessness and evil. In reality, it suddenly can seem more honest to hate then to love. In many crises, lies and indifference can be a more adequate response than truth and engagement. The human being who can lie well enough to be believed is a better man/woman in some situations that those who cannot; one here can have in mind situations of torture in war or a similar type of situation. Those who can hate so that it is noticeable *could* act as something of a wake-up call for another human being than those who without engagement accept the one.

Perhaps the most incomprehensible; because many people live in the world of shadows and believe that it is reality, they will fear what is positive. To accept the positive implies a complete overhaul of a lifestyle and deep attitudes. Happiness becomes a threat. Hope becomes depressing. Joy is to get affirmation of all that is dark and awful.

Despite all of this, those who confuse a world of shadows with reality might dream of the positive. But instead of trying to make everything real, they will make everything sentimental. They will put it into museums and dream about it as history and utopia. The happy childhood, the beloved departed, the prince who never comes, the millennium; all such dreams and notions serve something that complements their grey and bitter existence. Some oases filled with the positive are needed so that a negative reality can have meaning. None have as many happy dreams about people as those who see oppression everywhere.

Upon closer examination, the horizon is revealed as just as ambivalent and complex as intimate reality. Completely dependent on one's particular life and lifestyle, it will vary in character and content, be obvious as a parallel contradiction to reality here and now.

To live in relation to both reality and the horizon is to choose to live in uncertainty, where uncertainty can periodically imply security. As relates to the horizon and reality, that which is, and the complementary opposite, we have to shuttle back and forth and choose. This means living in a both-and paradigm, and then choosing in the depth of ourselves this both-and. In this process, phases of the either-or are not completely ruled out. Being either-or is part of both-and, but the opposite is not so.

We have to open up to the negative if we live one-sided in the positive and we must let in the positive if we live one-sided in the negative. Only then we can personalize our world, find our true engagements and get the inner self and the outer self to move. To talk about being whole means we have to take everything inside us and outside of us seriously.

Concretely, when relating to the horizon, many actions are possible, depending on what partial reality one determines to be true. But generally, it will mean seeking out all that is contradictory, different, and deviant. One is together with people who are very different from oneself, seek milieus outside of the usual, read unaccustomed literature and strive to gain a relationship to what has been rejected and despised. One tries to listen to those with whom one believes one disagrees with, and argue now and then against one's own points of view and oneself. One attempts to go against prejudice, become acquainted with what or whom one cannot tolerate. One strives to expand one's boundaries without becoming borderless and worthless. This implies that one is more spontaneous, open to new experiences, show trust and curiosity towards the world's many possibilities. The person lives in dialogue with his/her horizon.

Doing and Fighting

Dedication to personalizing processes is not only about experiencing new things, finding something new, and true, and beautiful, and admiring the horizon.

It also involves saying no, setting boundaries, fighting. One of the first things one has to say no to and to shut out is the impersonal. We have to be clear about what areas this belongs to and what it doesn't belong to. Testing boundaries does not mean dissolving them. We have to learn how to use our roles, make use of the impersonal, and to rest in the a-personal.

In the world of personalism, roles can only have a function if at least one of two conditions is met.

The first is that there is a *concrete task* that has to be carried out, something that applies to many careers and everyday situations. The relationship between people is determined by the tasks that they shall accomplice together.

The second condition, for roles to be legitimate is that in *relation to the task or purpose* of being together there exist no real equality between the persons. The one in that particular situation is wiser, more skilled, better and has more power than the other. Both of these conditions should occur simultaneously.

Dealing with impersonal roles in this case can be more merciful than clearly demonstrating the difference between persons and the minimal value of the fellowship.

One could take refuge in the impersonal as a form for rest. One can relax inside of the conventions and conversations, experience togetherness with people without having to make any effort. Being a person is often the same as lifting oneself by the hair, and that is a little too much at times. We therefore need the impersonal. However, at the moment one experiences conventions as exhausting, the impersonal as oppressive or nauseating, at that moment, it is time to change course and network, to renew the fight for your personal world.

In longer periods of time one can live in the impersonal, if there is a creative process going on inside that is not finished or ready to express. We also need time to play, time to be lazy. "Laziness is a time of growth," said *Friedrich von Schlegel*.[55]

We need situations where we are indecisive, seem to be no one, do not distinguish ourselves at anything nor have an opinion about anything at all. If we experience this harmoniously, then the person inside can grow. The person is always organically present anyway, always a possibility.

The impersonal, therefore has value as a tool or hiding place for the personal, when it is in the service of the personal. The person must decide for him/herself when and he/she can use the impersonal for something that is good, true, or beautiful.

The impersonal can also function to help developing useful routines and habits, spontaneity cannot be sustained forever, but must be regulated by a series of variable rules.

But in most situations, even those where it can be unclear what is really going on, the impersonal has to be battled against as the destructive force that it is. It is better to take one fight too many, than one too few. Some will maintain that it is of no use. Only a genuine attempt can tell us whether we can possibly make improvements. Our natural indolence and reserve will often be the main reason that we are hindered from shaping qualitatively truer and better interpersonal spaces.

When together with people, family, friends, acquaintances, colleagues and strangers, one has continually strives to communicate, mediate the self openly and decentralized, and expect that others will do the same. Should roles become too expansive in our existence, they will threaten the person and the person's sense of reality.

There will always be a chance in the nearest hour to eliminate roles and conventional answers and reactions, artificiality and falsehood, always new possibilities to be and to express the self.

In confrontation with the impersonal, the person becomes distinct, viewed against a background, the person gains a silhouette, and contours, for others and for the self. In the personal confrontation itself, the individual becomes a person. It is not one simple, isolated action, but many, endless ones. The personalizing processes are infinite and continue for as long as people are alive.

The ceaselessly personalizing processes will unavoidably lead to the development of personality and a far better life for those implicated.

The Art of the Dialogue

To personalize is not least of all learning to communicate, learning the art of the dialogue. In many ways, this can be viewed as the crystallization of the work to find the good, the true and the beautiful. The other person can be viewed as the horizon and communicating can be viewed as acting and fighting.

In our society, we can understand many of the problems of human beings as expressions for collapses in communication, whether on the inner or outer plane. Welfare diseases that are the result of a standard of living that is too comfortable can be viewed as bad communication between human beings and their own bodies. The ordinary consciousness doesn't grasp the body's signals; modern human beings cannot listen to inward themselves. Psychological problems can also be viewed in this light. Neuroses and obsessions are signs of inner constipation; at one point, the human being quit communicating with the self and with reality. Perceptions, feelings, and reactions are ignored, and inner communication is blocked and suppressed. Perhaps this happens because one does not want to start with any honest communication with one's surroundings, which is necessary for shedding light on the break in the inner communications.

To assert that people don't know themselves, really means that they don't communicate with themselves, they have ceased to converse with themselves. Consequently, it is not strange that they do not communicate well with others. To stay healthy and vigorous, a person simply has to participate in an ongoing conversation with the body and inner self.

Communication is the nature of the person; the human nature. Therefore, the experience of loneliness is completely natural; we cannot express our nature or communicate each time. Sometimes we have to do something else, work, sleep, and eat. And because it is everyone's nature to communicate, it can easily get crowded in a life together; everyone has a deep need to get the opportunity to say something, be heard, and get reactions. For these two reasons, communication becomes necessarily difficult.

But communication can never be some kind of technique or method. We can't develop routines to ensure that people will communicate with themselves and each other satisfactorily. The reason for this is that there are other aspects of human nature that create some almost insurmountable problems, problems that will always be there when two people meet. Some of that has been mentioned earlier. Let me expand on the most important problems.

The first problem can be blamed on the personal, or rather, the inscrutability in the person. This foreign, mystical, diffuse, will always ensure that there is something we cannot quite understand about each other. We can easily feel that we can't get to bottom of things, that there is something hidden from us, that the other is secretive.

We thereby feel a distance. The distance will foster a feeling of insecurity, and insecurity will create anxiety. Then, communication, the fellowship, easily breaks down.

The second problem can be due to the person's uniqueness. All of us are something to ourselves. If this cannot be integrated and understood, there is fertile soil for the experience of something strange, distance, and a breakdown in communication.

Two other problems that are just as disturbing come from the mass man/woman. When people appear to be like and behave just like all the others the excitement of communication disappears. One starts to get bored and quits listening closely, reacts on catchwords to deliver one's own rejoinders. The communication stiffens and dies.

The same thing happens if people behave as if all the others are like them. If people talk as if all experiences are common ones: 'just wait until you get as old as I am or come into a situation that resembles the one I am in, then you too will. . .' they kill communication. It becomes impossible because the differences in experiences hinder it, and the similar experiences make it uninteresting.

The individual's inclination to always stand outside, to always create outburst and rebellion makes it almost an impossible conversation partner. The individual forces others to be passive listeners; it imperialistic forces its own world on others.

A variety of normal opinions can also create problems in communicating. There are many forms of reductionism; phenomena are reduced to something less meaningful than they really are and their power is removed. Some people see all communication as chat; some care only about some parts of the message, whether it is words or feelings. And then others think that nothing is important enough to talk about or that the important things cannot be talked about. Or they think that all people are thoroughly boring.

And naturally, the emptier people try to be, the emptier the lives they lead; the more difficult it will be to start a real conversation with them, a proper conversation.

Should one wish to be good at communicating, it is precisely these problems with which one must work. The best place to start is always with oneself.

Everyone can think about what they usually talk about with others, and the way they do it. Then they can ask themselves different questions.

One central question is whether one is clever enough to distinguish between *the private* and *the personal*. If one talks with other people only about what one yourself have experienced, without making any attempt to look at it in a greater and more all-encompassing connection, one is speaking privately. Describing pain, emotions and experience so that others can immerse themselves in them, only poets can do, and that is best done in writing. On the other hand, one can describe the situation itself so that others can recognize it, and add new moments. One can develop the conversation to discuss something general and universal; talk about the reasons for sicknesses and the way that society treats them instead of all the thousand tiny details of the body. Instead of talking about grandchildren, one can talk about children's situation in society.

One must also use a language that offers space for others to speak, should one desires communication. This also applies to the rules for the situation itself. One does not speak privately, out of the window, but to someone who participates. Communication is to be face-to-face; looking at each other, and experience each other in a common room. If there is not room for all, make room.

The private world is perhaps communication's worst enemy. Many people who feel that no one ever understands them are perhaps people who always speak privately and *can* therefore never be understood. Others can exhibit sympathy, but the one-sided individual complaining makes communication impossible.

Generally, the most successful theme will be that which offers both parties space in a greater context, without it being impossible for the subjective to be thought in. The exchange between the general and the universal and the individual can allow the personal to be expressed.

Since communication is sharing something, make common, it is important to be clear about what can be made common in the given situation. This responsibility belongs to both, to all partners.

It is also important to be clear about the fact that communication is not a discontinued, final, and unambiguous act. The inscrutable must be accepted in order to give depth to communication. Communication with others continues to live in us; we have to give attention to the passing time. No one can say everything at a particular point in time; our understanding has to be open for new understandings. We have to let words and sentences live in us; communication must be allowed to develop even after we have left one another. This means to give room for the other as a person. The other one shall live in us even when that person is not physically present. The words of the other are viewed in a variety of meanings; their opinions are experienced as sketches for our worldview.

Communication is first and foremost a process and, as such, it is like processes that occur in nature and not in a test tube. Communication is to express wholeness, including those that relate to the future and all those others as yet unknown.

It is also an ethical task and a challenge. That those who resemble each other also understand each other is no achievement. Neither is it any great feat to continuously offer witty comments, or just prattle away about almost anything.

It is good will, sensitivity, impartiality, evaluation, reason and linguistic fantasy, and variation that transform people into good conversation partners. One gains skills in communication through different personalizing exercises.

We can work on our courage by what we truly feel and think more often. This means picking a fight with the tyranny of hurt feelings. The anxiety around hurting someone is often really about our own anxiety for expressing ourselves, thereby losing popularity. Or the anxiety for the reactions we may get from others. Or the anxiety for real communication; it is far easier to converse than to communicate.

We can exercise our ability to understand diversity, both where words, feelings and actions are concerned.

Everyday philosophizing can also help communication. The ability to ask questions like a child: How? Why? Where?. . . at the right time and wrong time can help both ability to listen and fantasy.

And two people can help each other to practice and be like the scholars in the middle ages. They choose some blazing topic, and each listens to the other's point of view, until the listener is able to interpret the viewpoint of the speaker, so that he/she accepts the other's interpretation. The condition for practicing the ability to communicate is that each party has positions that are far apart from the other, preferably the opposite viewpoint. The goal is not that they should change positions or that they should agree but be able to understand each other and recognize position of the other in the debate.

Should there be two parties in a love relationship and friendship, the test is more exciting and fruitful. Some people will discover that they are not as diametrically opposed to each other as they thought; lack of communication can often be lack of proper knowledge about the other's viewpoint and language. Everyday small tragedies happen when people make mistakes concerning disagreements, gaining more opponents than necessary. To make a mistake where agreements are concerned can just as well result in tragedies in more rarely instances.

Communication, like the nature of the person, is so central to us that we can say that we cease to be a person when we do not communicate. Then communication is understood as both an inner and an outer process. Should this process, this dialogue that emerges from one's own body and mind, other people and, from greater metaphysical parts and ideas, discontinue, then the human being becomes either a mass man/woman or an individual. Both are characterized by a lack of communication, mass man makes it into an illusion, private talk on a group level, while the individual makes in into private talk on an individual plane. The person's unceasing desire for dialogue demonstrates how the person is the real human being; the mass man and the individual simply bad copies.

Chapter VII

Housekeeping of the Person

PERSONALIST PHILOSOPHY CANNOT BE used to benefit either a socialist view of humanity or a conservative. It is also unlikely that politically interested people would see how such thinking is relevant.

The reason for this is that most politicians do not see the value of ethics. To the contrary, politics is often viewed as a recess from ethics and morality. Nonetheless, all healthy politics of course depend on people who have their ethics intact.

As a rule, talking about morals is a bit like waving a red flag. Why this should be so is hard for me to understand. Perhaps there are many who can't stand the thought that at any time they might not be viewed the same as or better than others? Or because they in reality have given up their own growth and do not like to be reminded that others still struggle to move forward? Or could it be that they have a deep anxiety for taking responsibility?

Perhaps this aggression emerges because ethics separates people into different categories; some is considered to be better than others. In a society with equality as its foundation, this is outrageous. Just as in principle people are supposed to have the same material conditions, they should also have the same spiritual conditions. But spirit and ethics cannot be distributed by the state.

This is something that people give to themselves, through their lives and actions. Anyone, can behave ethically, anyone can strive to improve their morals, and quality of life. Everybody has to do this on our own, alone.

To me, it is clearly necessary to distinguish between different phases and different lifestyles. Mass man, individuals, and persons are not equally good, not equally equipped to create a good and democratic society, they are not equally comfortable.

A lack of distinctions when human quality is concerned weakens the possibility to work towards good and spiritual values. If we think about all people as equally good in themselves, and view evil as simply a result of society, state, or coincidence, then the human being becomes a victim, nobody. Then we prevent perception, discussion, and critique of values. We can no longer sense what we experience, nor analyze realties.

We can neither dream about our own growth. The distinction does not run just between people we meet and know, but also within us. If we are to deny the importance of moral ideals and standards, then we also have to deny that we ourselves are not equally good from day to day. Then we assert values-nihilism, even in our own development. All that we do, whether it is good or evil, is becomes equally valuable. This inevitably leads to inner emptiness.

Therefore, we have to repeatedly ask about motives, actions, and patterns in life, first and foremost our own, but others. This is to prevent evil, indifference, narrow-mindedness, and the impersonal from gaining too much importance in our lives. We must constantly work to improve our existence and be ready to confront others when necessary. Since our lives are always shared, there is no one who lives a solitary life.

Morality: The Source of Engagement

We can relate to moral challenge in at least three ways. We can give up completely, and just complain about the weakness and misery of humanity. Or we can be indifferent to others, and care for ourselves. But as a *person*, we must accept the challenges and work hard to communicate and to confront.

Morals create energy and offer faith and hope. Human beings with clear ideas about a *worthy life* will also have possibility to improve their lives. And a human being who knows deep down that he/she has behaved well and done something to be proud of will feel a sense of inner security, and the need to make an even greater effort. Courage grows. When morals have an effect like this, it comes not from feelings of lust and random needs, but instead is founded on conceptualization of the whole and on free will.

Morality has a unique dimension that can't be reduced or transformed into something else. We can never avoid asking whether what is happening inside us and outside us is good or evil. We can never let others answer these questions or find some kind of outer, unambiguous measure. We must always support our answers directly in our own experiences.

What everyone else may choose is not necessarily good; *mass man/ woman* is no ethical measure. They choose what is good just as readily as they choose what is bad if sufficiently motivated. The public can have good taste as well as bad, and whatever is trendy at the time can have quality, but just as often not. Random and deeper subconscious powers are in control.

The individual is also sparingly committed to morals, he/she will choose whatever suits them best and promote that in their relationship to the masses. If it thinks that morality is the norm for the masses, it will if necessary place itself in a position above morals. The individual is not able to judge anything according to common ethical standards.

We can neither use feelings to judge whether something is good or evil. That which wound other human beings is not necessarily evil, or what give them joy good. In many societies, the quality of interpersonal relationships can be severely damaged by the tyranny of hurt feelings. Much that is meaningful is unsaid or left undone due to the anxiety that someone's status or vanity may be hurt. The demand for friendliness, conceal interpersonal realities. When one has to be nice and cozy, there can be a lot of aggression stored away, and avoidance of confrontation. As a result, both rebellion and reconciliation becomes impossible, true inter-subjectivity never develop. In these kinds of environments, people are inevitable strangers to one another.

When we experience reality ethically, we can see that much we at once thought is good is evil, and what we believe is evil will finally been revealed as good. Aggression, a blow, perhaps even a theft or murder might be good in one situation, an unselfish act, like turning the other cheek, could be evil in another situation. Moralists set automatic standards.

People who lack ethical experience, or who due to shame, bad conscious and hate, do their best to suppress any such experience and will have energy to change only if consumed by pride, hunger for power, or envy. Their feelings are in the driver seat. It could be said that their feelings walk in front of them and drag them along.

With true ethical experiences as basis one gets both support and guidance. By the power of the ethical experience itself, one can maximize the good and minimize the bad. Just as experience of love, makes one happy, generous, and selfless.

The Significance of the Creative Wills

In the moral act something new is entering the world. By such an act accepted patterns and norms changes. By intervening on behalf of justice, through honoring and keeping holy all that has value, by acting for the good and the true, the world changes, a new understanding penetrates situations and transforms both the situation and the participants.

There are many reasons to cherish fantasy, spontaneity, and creativity. The most important reason is that they represent the conditions for ethical actions. In most situations, we will need everything associated with the creative to be able to act ethically.

The positive ethical behavior is never rote, never depicted beforehand or portrayed in a book or any set of rules. Even the Ten Commandments contain mainly just what one should refrain from doing. For to refrain from or avoid an action does not require spontaneity or fantasy; it requires self-control and restraint. Indeed, most ethical demands concern *not avoiding action*. They involve how we *should act*, how to intervene when action is required. In most situations, one won't have time to judge whether it is proper to act. If one witnesses a beating or a threat to someone, one can't first confer with the police to find out what one should do.

This is why the conventional man/woman can be a threat to morals. He/she have learned that they shouldn't get mixed up in other people's private lives and that it is societal institutions that shall seek justice and ethical quality in interpersonal relationships. If he/she shall be able to engage in something new and act for the good, they must first part company with their upbringing and be prepared to live without too rigid conventions.

Indifference means that people live only inside their conventions and act according to already established patterns. Only personalizing of their existence can remove indifference; then can people see existence as open to spontaneous, creative actions of own self.

While bad morals in our society for the most part is absence of action, pure sins of omission, only deep wickedness needs action, then, good moral is actions that require spontaneity and a creative will.

In order to be good, one has to want it, have the will for goodness, and the courage to stand up alone if necessary. What one should do, everyone has to figure out for him or herself in the very moment that one acts. The good deed is its own justification. In the second that it occurs, it defends and legitimizes itself. Doubt usually means that the deed is not a good one.

The creative will is in fact just as necessary for the moral human being as for the artist. The mental creative act, the desire for what is good, is completely central to the good deed. All people will need to develop their creative ability; to be able to create becomes a precondition for being good. The intentional, creative artist can be a model for a good human being.

During the creative act, the will and the senses are united. One attempts both to let something grow and to form it with one's thought, both in receiving and giving of self and of the artistic object. To be mentally creative is therefore to look into new worlds, to meet the unknown and confront the old and often powerful. Being creative demands that one is able to live with angst and uncertainty and to dare realize dreams.

During the creative process qualities that add value to the good moral act thus become clear. One practices concentration, which means that one sees reality instead of delusions, see what is really happening, not least of all when it is outside the road most traveled and not noticed. One exercises effort and devotion. The act, or piece of art, will follow.

The vital happens; love for what is good arises. The good becomes both a dream and a reality, and giving it shape and form becomes an absolute necessity. To act is to shape goodness. The good human being must live in close proximity to the good, continually maximize it, and continue to see the good deed as one of his or her many children that may cause some trouble. But just as a work of art has affects, and has to make it on its own, so in the same way, must the good deed also make it.

Morals are humanity's first work of art. We are all each other's dreams, each other's tools and materials for a good life, each other's challenging reality. If good cannot be found in creative acts, it cannot be found at all.

Generosity: A Rule of Life

Each human being can choose the personal, ethics and love, no matter what type of society and environment, family, others, and strangers.

The choice is therefore to develop that distinct economic principle that belongs to the person, *generosity*. Generosity implies qualities such as *hospitality, magnanimity, reciprocity, openness, benevolence*, and the ability to *forgive*.

Generosity was deeply valued in old agricultural societies. One's guest was well cared for, shown respect, and honor, and oneself felt honored by the visit. The interests of the guest were one's own; the guest became the center of attention and was supposed to feel that way. The host and his/her guest became a unit, anyone who insulted a guest, insulted the host as well. Between the host and the guest, a fellowship developed, as long as the visit lasted.

As the word *generosity* implies, along with ones attitudes and actions, one gives other gentle gifts: friendliness, smiles, small favors, warmth and something of oneself in each situation, care in the intimate and daily life. Gentleness will heal and unite, reconcile and mediate, become a bridge from one human being to another human being. Generosity is common; the generous does not think about those who are favored have deserved his/her gentle gift or not.

Reciprocity implies first and foremost the will to do return. The fundamental reciprocity in relation to others means that in one's own life one is willing to make a space for others, willing to accept the possibility for a committed relationship. One receives something from others, and one wants to give back. But it is not like a trade. What one gives does not have to be the same as what one receives, or at the same time, and it may even be something different. When one of the parties gives money, the other can give attention, when one gives understanding, the other can give something useful. The point is that one allows oneself to be committed to somebody, in some kind of context, to accept that one is in relationship to the other. Reciprocity in this sense becomes an acknowledgment of the fundamental importance of the interpersonal, and that each relationship should be expressed, manifested in some way. In reciprocity, the 'I' acknowledges the 'Thou'.

By only receiving, is to stand outside the relationship. The same happens if one is insisting on always being the one who gives. When someone chooses to either give only or receive only, they are clearly saying that they do not wish a personal relationship.

According to the conventions of the day, this kind of give and take has been reduced to a kind of bartering; one must contribute according to what one receive, preferably something that is directly comparable to what you have received. We ought to give approximately as expensive Christmas and birthday presents. A suitable amount of time after being invited to an event, one should invite back. As a result, it is difficult if not impossible to feel that one can really give or receive something, one gives with the thought of receiving and receive with the thought of what you will be given. The expectations from others ruin the joy of what one has received. Such gifts and contributions create more emptiness than pleasure and do not establish generosity.

In such cases the relationship is disintegrated into things and contributions of various types. But the symbols of the relationship are not the relationship itself; reciprocity is a duty based on past experiences in the relationship. The thousands of things and contributions do not necessarily result in a personal relationship, even if they are regularly distributed.

Sincerity finds its origins in generosity. To give of oneself, one's honest and heartfelt reactions, shows who one really is, is a way to broaden existence for others, enrich them, add something that is different and new compared to who they are themselves. And simultaneously, one receive from the other and becomes enriched with his/hers experiences and points of view regarding existence.

Forbearance also works to expand the world. No need to feel ashamed, to regret, to be embarrassed, there is breathing space and the possibility for progress. To bear over, *carry* the weaknesses of others, can also make one more tolerant of one's own weaknesses. And it tells that one acknowledges that one's and others experiences are more and perhaps even completely different than what one assumes in the moment. This means also to lift the experience into a higher plane and make it richer. Those who are overbearing, see possibilities, promise, in others and in the self, and in the relationships.

Forgiveness has the same effect. To be forgiven is to be able to move on, no longer be stuck in some old patterns, living as if trapped in a reality that is past and no longer has possibilities of actions. True forgiveness allows the other to develop, express and start to communicate again. It restores the relationship, sets it free. As a result, the one who forgives is also released; for the inability to forgive results in being blocked. The inability to forgive blocks one's own life processes and one regards a relationship only in light of one of many possible actions.

That forgiveness at times can be impossible, and perhaps not even appropriate, does not refute this truth. Sometimes blocking can be the only realistic way forward. Lack of forgiveness can be a way creating the self. And in the same way, when forgiveness in not truly and deeply felt, no one is liberated.

The economy of the person, the person's affairs, allows everyone to be persons; it shares reality amongst those present. Generosity, the horn of plenty that the personality possesses, creates respect, freedom, makes room for the other, and sets up both the inner and the outer fellowship. To develop the personality is to develop the self so that you become enriched, have plenty of space in one's mind and life for all the possibilities in oneself and in others.

Love's Conditions

It has often been said that love in our modern welfare state has bad conditions. This refers to the kinds of attitudes and values that an economy based on money and personal competition produces. If love is going to be able to survive in this hunt for status and possessions, it requires an effort that few modern people are willing to make. Subconsciously, they expect that love will be served to them, and that love is a birthright or something to barter with.

Perhaps it is true that the conditions love makes are seldom fulfilled. But one could just as easily assert that modern man is unable to love. If one only blames society, one can easily overlook the fact that more than anything else, love is personal creation; love comes into existence almost out of nothing when two people meet.

When faced with the choice that all people must make, namely the choice of whether to be a mass man, an individual or a person, most will choose one of the two first. With these choices, they choose not to love. Neither the mass man/woman nor the individual *can* be successful in love affairs, talking about love quickly becomes a self-contradiction to them.

Mass man's kind of love is fleeting and superficial, largely pure pleasure. Mass man/woman enjoys either the other human being, sexually or esthetically, or enjoys being the object of someone else's love. Sexual desire forces them to seek out others, but only in order to satisfy physical needs. The other party's beauty or material success in the masses is also part of the attraction, becomes like a favorite painting or a card to all of the finest clubs and gatherings that society has to offer. The relationship to others is dominated by use, it is practical to have a partner, to have children, to achieve one's daily work, to be supported and taken care of. Seen in this way, mass man/woman accepts love as a relationship of much joy.

In many ways, mass man seeks the end of desire. The deepest wish is to eat, drink and love until empty, enjoy the boundlessness and eternal qualities of nothingness.

To the degree that mass man can live in love, it dominated by narcissism, he/she loves their own image in the mirror, the self in the other. Mass man falls in love with the other party's infatuation for him or her rather than in that person. Neither the other party nor the self is viewed as anything special, any theory about love revolves around the natural world or emerges out of egotism. Love is quite trivial.

The beginning of a relationship is expressed by conventional rituals, and likewise romance is often defined by external symbols such as red roses and gold rings; femininity and masculinity are expressed first and foremost through tertiary sexual characteristics; make up, red nails, clothes and snappy comebacks. The one and only great love is manifested by the white bridal gown and chivalry. For mass man, the relationship is dissolved into things and symbols, the props and sets. The relationship has to look successful from the outside and needs to be accepted by others as properly executed. Only when the appearances of the relationship measure up can mass man identify what has been experienced and offer his or her emotions.

Mass man/woman cannot learn what love is, because he/she only acknowledges what is part of him or her, what belongs to him or her. The world's boundaries end with the self. He/she doesn't believe in the unique human being. Self-righteousness permeates their entire being and view of humanity. Mass man emphasizes the profane as an ideal and cultivates one singular copy of humanity, him or herself.

Mass man/woman can never be creative in any situation. That would mean stepping outside of the ranks, becoming something different than others, which is unthinkable. There is no desire to do anything of the sort, and should such thoughts be entertained, he/she becomes afraid. The beloved never becomes a 'you' in his/her eyes, never becomes appreciable from any of the others in the same group and the same environment. The mass man's sweetheart is a representative for a specific group and never gains more distinction and life than anyone else. That is why the many interchangeable partners will resemble each other and have the same roles and functions.

The love relationships of mass man/woman, is dominated by conventions, other people's expectations, and a predetermined way of life. Love is never a break with life, never a provocation, and never a revolution as *Alberoni* claims it should be in his book *Falling in Love and Love*.[56] That is why mass man grows bored with love after a while. In order to get some excitement in life, there has to be a search for it outside of the love relationship for other partners, being unfaithful gives the illusion of being a separate "I," divorce becomes one of life's dramatic high points. Such drama means that in the next relationship, he/she will seek more deeply inside the masses, choose partners that offer more social safety. The foundation of the existence can be found only in the middle of the crowd, either literally since there is an inability to relate to quiet and peace but a continuous search for the type of activity that gives one the feeling of belonging, or symbolically by never doing more than is expected. Nothing happens in the middle of the crowd. There is simply the illusion of that.

Correspondingly, the *individual* is also incapable of love. It wants love only so that someone will call attention to him/her, exalt them, admire them, like a woman dreaming about meeting her prince so she will be visible to others and the eyes of society, or how a man dreams about a woman as his muse. The individual's love object has the task of working relentlessly to deliver the beloved, to help the beloved achieve immortality, and to elevate his or her status in society. All that is unique about the individual can be found with the other. The individual wants more than anything to be loved by a partner who has a more elevated social status, longs more to be loved than to love.

But the individual never loves anyone other him/herself. Its love is not necessarily limitless narcissistic. For no one else can resemble the individual and the need for love is primarily a need for a public and support on the way to the top or into history.

The individual's ability, to keep holy or to recognize that someone or something may be greater or better than he/she, is not developed. The individual bows only in honor of his or her own greatness and lives the whole life yearning to see it come to pass, meaning recognition from others. The individual is disappointed in his or her love affairs quickly and easily. Partners don't offer appropriate admiration when they are present and may even demand admiration and support for themselves. This is something that the individual can accept only if the implicit understanding is that he or she is the better and greater. Should any problems arise in the relationship, the individual will increase demands to the other, the other is the one who needs to change, accept to be next best.

Such attitudes naturally can only create imbalanced relationships, the other gender in the eyes of the individual, seems inferior, undeveloped, immature and domineering, but also maybe the opposite. The individual cannot individualize others and regards all other men or women as cut from the same cloth. Relationships break apart quickly, become largely unequal and dominated by a lack of equality, or become eternal power struggles.

Accordingly the individual can use love affairs symbolically in order to be successful. By struggling against and perhaps overpowering the other, the individual gains a small pedestal on which to stand over the masses. Relationships can be useful to the individual, standing on someone else with or without permission from the other means standing a head higher than at least one other in the masses. Having someone to decide over means they are one step closer to their own individualization. This is why having children is a major step for the individual. Through children they become greater and more than just one. Not having someone, not even children, is to be on the bottom, the lowest, one of the masses. Psychological problems in connection with childlessness can be an expression of anxiety for the masses, for leaving the world just as unnoticed as living in it.

Should individuals fail in their efforts for love, they become cynical. They then declare that love is impossible, an illusion, just romance and nonsense for teenagers. Should they speak of love, it is an implied reduction; love is only this or that, only eroticism, only attraction, only use, only need, only chemical reactions. The individual always see all the others and other relationships as 'only.' This *only* fosters indifference and in the final analysis, emptiness, powerlessness, and helplessness.

Mass man and the individual have completely opposite problems, where love relationships are concerned. While mass man fails because he or she is no one, cannot be loved, cannot be visible, but is only a shadow of the others, the individual fails because he or she is the only one, too much of a good thing, and incapable of love. There is a dark and threatening shadow over all of the relationships that they live in, also friendships. Others are invisible in their presence.

Neither mass man nor the individual can live in real relationships simply because both lack of human reality. When one of the parts is not a person, is not real, then the relationship is dead. Only the work to personalize one's existence can add content to the relationship.

Only *persons* can love and be loved. Love means that there are two loving and loveable people. *Both* sees the other as truly unique, manages to be partners in an "I-you" relationship, each receives and gives love with generosity and each will remain ethically creative in the relationship in the years ahead.

Only the person can satisfy the conditions of love. The person is humble enough to yield to love as a power all its own, a blessing that comes from above. Love becomes a law that must be followed. It is also only the person who is creative enough to experience his or her own self and experience the whole of the other, sees the 'you' just as well as they see the 'I.' Only the person can experience human existence as a unique dimension.

Perhaps most importantly, only the person is able to keep communication alive in the self and the relationship for long as the relationship lasts. Only death can separate the lovers from one another.

There are many who would say that love demands quite a bit

And yet, it is little enough really, it is much less than that which all of the impersonal relationships demand of the masses and the individuals should we be able to judge by the number of divorces and the agonizing battles over parental rights to children, marriages that have developed into something destructive, and the number of lonely people who do not live in close relationships at all. These relationships demand long periods of loneliness, enmity, destruction, lack of balance and equality, isolation, lack of communication, no real conversations, and sincere meetings. They demand stereotypical opinions and roles, rejection of goodness and friendliness—in short, the ability to do what little is needed, and even less, the ability to reduce and lessen, to work against hope and optimism. In our society, disappointed people use a lot of energy to rationalize their right to be disappointed, thereby increasing their susceptibility for disappointments.

And if love demands much, miserliness, pettiness, hate, indifference, superficial connections and the impersonal thus don't demand less.

Blaming society and complaining about the conditions that love sets is to completely forget that love, like generosity, is a quality of the single human being, and not systems and large groups. It exists only in personal meetings, and there only. The existential reality and the social belong to two completely different dimensions or aspects of a human being's life. To love or to develop the personal is to exceed, to tear oneself loose from the grip that society has on you through the singular ethical act of creation. Each step forward is difficult and, quite naturally, should be so.

Sexual Liberation

The challenges that love presents in Western societies, one has since the fifties and sixties, attempted to nullify with the so-called sexual revolution. It should no longer be necessary to love each time one made love; the revolution consisted in the freedom of bodies and sex organs to meet without any obligation. While old-fashioned, monogamous marriage placed little value on erotic feelings, especially those of women, and gladly separated love from eroticism, the sexual revolution placed little value on love, especially for men. Consequently, the sexual revolution became a mirror image of earlier times; the deep division between love and eroticism was kept. The result was that the vulgarity of human relationships continued.

Narcissistic modern man is responsible for this perpetuation of the vulgarity. Narcissus was the man who loved himself so much that he became lost in his own image. In modern psychoanalysis, the narcissist is the man/woman that is the entire center of his/her own activities, cultivates him/herself and view all others as surrogates and objects for their own use. They inhabit a false self and are unable to experience their own ego. They remain in inner isolation, an inner prison.

There are no boundaries between the narcissist and others. Should the others, the object, refuse to function as objects, the narcissist is gripped with an intense rage. When he/she loses control, the outbursts of aggression are completely uninhibited. The narcissistic swing back and forth between grandiose notions about he/herself and depression, and develop authoritarian, totalitarian façades as a protection from their own inner emptiness.

The assumption is that the narcissistic has been unable to develop emotional lives. It will not dare to feel anything, especially not negative, spontaneous feelings directed towards parents, especially the mother. If it should dare to do that, he/she would be confronted with rejection and the parents' real, perhaps indifferent feelings.

The narcissistic individual has forbidden him/herself to acknowledge feelings. At the same time, he/she will often try to reestablish their childhood dramas; the intellectual life will be overdeveloped as compensation. We find an empty, frightened and opportunistic individual, blind to the boundaries between the I and the Thou. They cultivate the collective as compensation since they are unable to experience people as unique and deeply different from one another. Or they cultivate themselves without ability to experience that other people exist.[57]

Both mass man and the individuals can be narcissistic. The difference is mass man's cultivation of its own group, blind both to the distinctive qualities of other groups as well as their right to exist, and the individual's cultivation of only him/herself. Narcissism has both a collectivist and an individualistic side.

Sexual liberation can be viewed as a narcissistic movement. Others must be available as objects, give purely physical pleasure. Ideas developed that it was a right of modern human beings to expect such pleasure from others; if you didn't embrace promiscuity, you were seen as inhibited, puritanical, frigid, or impotent. The pleasure was all that mattered. All boundaries were to be obliterated. Even your own gender became a possible object for extraordinary pleasure. The homosexual liberation movement followed the sexual liberation movement.

That the sexual revolution in reality had little to do with eroticism, we see in the vulgarization and emptiness. The idea of pleasure became its only idea. We did not get developed the idea about the essential feminine or the essential masculine, or the idea about love as fate. Pleasure was seen in isolation; it made no difference who and what induced it or what the results were. The culture of intoxication is another result of all of this. And perhaps not the least of all, basic elementary taboos disappeared or were ridiculed. Anything was permitted, also all that gave dimensions to human relationships. Existence became unbearably boring.

No one gets heart palpitations from doing what no one will scold them for doing or refrain from doing. But we need to live in an interaction with taboos in order to be torn out of boredom. Taboos are centers of power, loaded with either divine or satanic power. Perhaps the only exciting experience there is, is to *approach* a taboo. To break with a taboo takes the power out of existence.

The modern narcissistic human being lives without taboos. Therefore, he/she also live without love, without the fateful that love for another human being can mean. And he/she doesn't experience the deep drama between the eternal feminine and the eternal masculine. In the erotic meeting between one man and one woman arises a relationship loaded with power, struggle, and fate. It is love within eroticism, and the eroticism in love that shakes the personal worlds.

Some of what was lost in the sexual revolution and in its wake was the experience itself of sex, especially the opposite sex. With this I do not mean the qualities that the sexes are usually proscribed; manly strength, activity and hardness contrasted with female weakness, passivity and softness.

I mean the experience of a man as man and a woman as woman. Even in these days of equal rights, for women it is this experience that lends excitement and drama to love. Searching for one's beloved is also searching for the one of the opposite sex who appears to be more of a man or more of a woman than any other man and woman.

This fundamental experience of the opposite sex is not easy to express; any attempt at descriptions become full of keywords. The experience is irreducible; it only is, like the experience of oneself as a person. That is why it is so powerful, so intertwined with power and fate.

Sexual liberation brought no freedom. Where there is no place for love, or where it is depicted as something incidental that anyone can experience with anyone, the result is emptiness and chaos.

Freedom must always be won. Erotic freedom is no exception. Erotic liberation is the establishment of a living, perceptive, contentious, sensual relationship to the one who you actually love. It is that simple—and that difficult.

In order to do this, you have to be able to sense what is lasting, and has quality. It will always mean being able to perceive a person, a personality, not just a body, skin and hair. A central part of the love affair is the experience of being made for each other, being each other's man or woman. It is the experience that you yourself and the other, and the relationship, have quality. Or the experience of something unique, not just in the other person, or in you, but in the relationship itself that makes room for the lovers.

Sexual liberation offered freedom from the personal, presented an opportunity to forget who you were and that you didn't need to bother about who the other one was. It was unnecessary to ask about value, ethics or the ability to love, only about technique and positions during intercourse. You could thereby also avoid caring about personal growth and maturity. One could be a thing for amusement of others and oneself. The emphasis was placed on infatuation, the narcissist's only experience of love. It was not only about loving the 'one' in oneself, but also loving oneself in the other, or loving the other one's love for oneself. To love became loving to be loved. That is why promiscuity became a value of its own. Being loved by many became safety, reinforcing the idea that you were the most beautiful of all. Being loved by only one cannot convince the narcissist. For all of those who became promiscuous because it was fashionable, the experience must be like a boomerang, and even made it difficult for them to experience the unique character of love. Having had sex with so many others will be a disclaimer every time one enters into a new love relationship.

First and foremost, sexual liberation was a movement that opposed love, an attempt to neutralize the dramatic significance of love in the relationship between people and the sexes and in society in general.[58]

The Loving Person

Only the person can love. To be a person means, AMO ERGO SUM; I love, therefore I am. This creed of love is the fundamental acknowledgment of the main value of the relationship and the existence of the other. Only the person can perceive the existence of the other, the Thou. Understanding the other, the Thou as a living reality, is a condition for love. Simultaneously, it is love that makes you completely real to yourself, that gives you beyond all doubt assurance of your own existence.

The loving human being does not resemble the sugar-sweet, self-annihilating individual that popular Christianity usually promotes. Masochism and the wish to take on everyone's sin make no one into a loving being. "With the help of theology, we have turned this all upside down, so that people now learn to love each other *as little* as they are taught to love themselves."[59] Loving cannot be reduced to *suffering* blindly; a sacrifice has to have meaning and be worth something.

When a person grows, the ability to love is under development. The loving human being grows in the battle against the negative, impersonal daily challenges both in and outside of oneself.

Let me repeat the characteristics of the person: The personal shows itself in the ability to use the negative in service of the good, in the development of real dialogue. The person chooses daily between the impersonal and the personal, between evil and the good, the ambiguous and the complex, and chooses to be present with both body and soul, working consciously for universal values that promote the person as the highest value. It is here we will also find love.

The personal and the loving are merged into a separate, third dimension. It is expressed through many patterns and connections. Should mass man be the past and individual the future, then love is the immediate present. If the human being's society is chaos, or predetermined order, it is also a living order. If the human being can be used or mistreated as an object, described and analyzed or be hectic action, the observer or the participant, then the person can also meet and be met.

Erotic love, heterosexuality, is therefore one important source for the personal. In it, we meet the person as a lasting, psychophysical whole, complementary, foreign and excessive, the *second* sex. It is therefore a unique opportunity to experience the eternal "we," both as an expression for two persons, and as an expression for the mystical, the original, the entire creature, and the person who both is man and woman. That special meeting neutralizes, but does not remove, the danger of, the foreign, inscrutable and mystical.

In the sensual union between man and woman, the third dimension of the loving human being is illustrated. During intercourse, the two lovers are completely physically present; they both experience and share an experience. A new level is attained: presence. When skin meets skin, reality is not debatable and the boundaries between the two are dissolved. The boundaries can just as readily be one's own skin as the other's skin. Skin becomes an entrance, something that to some degree dissolves, the way the eye cannot catch glimpse the self, but makes room for impressions and things.

Not least of all, it is the well-developed sensuality that gives sexuality its wholeness and creativity. The entire human being becomes one great erogenous zone. The erotic works from the inside out; orgasm gains a new depth, and can no longer be compared to a sneeze of the kind *Inge and Sten Hegeler* wrote about in the sixties.[60] It has the depth of the sea, a cosmic experience of the kind described by *Wilhelm Reich*.[61] The experience adds insight to something that resembles creation, resurrection or the even the creator, himself: a total experience that is so complete it cannot be compared with anything else.

In the experience of orgasm, people can glimpse new depths and dimensions. The two lovers become a moving whole, the shared ecstasy makes them both surrender, and it is not possible to distinguish between the giver and the receiver. Something new comes into existence.

Eroticism is manifested as anything other than a need if by that one means a more or less physical instinct that people may have in common with animals. Hunger is not the same as experiencing a meal. In the same way, it is the experience of the beloved, the reciprocal relationship that creates erotic tension, and not coincidental and lonely physical desires. Eroticism has a place in a metaphysical personal reality.

In the sexual act, the person is clearly both the self and interwoven with the other. To be able to express oneself increase the intimate understanding of the other. In that deepest of fellowships, none of the persons allows their personalities to be dissolved.

In this erotic experience man and woman will affirm each other; experience each other as two parts of a whole. The relationship between the two becomes a conversation between differences that are both opposites and harmonic parallels.

Infatuation, even the narcissistic, also reveals something important about the loving person. When infatuated, daily life loses its meaning; the normal routines of eating and sleeping become unimportant. Daily routines and habits dissolve, and instead existence becomes a drama. In the center of the drama are the two lovers, their comings and goings, and the small things that happen can create divine happiness or desperate chaos. In this intoxication, the two are bound to one another, become each other's connection to reality.

For that matter, one could say that only through sensuality and love does the body become spirit; only the fully sensual body will be able to experience that it is something more than a body. Love is an invitation to a metaphysical leap, touching something other than mere body or the object for sensual experiences.

In this meeting, the human being is pulled out of the conditional and the contingent, but is also not lost in the universal and the necessary. In between the coincidental and the necessary, between pure body and pure spirit, something emerges that is so difficult to express, the living subject, the eternal in the present, a completely special dimension of meaning.

In love, the experience radically expands what it means to be human. This experience is irreversible. One becomes crystal clear, experiences the inner world as translucent, and sees both the dangerous reefs and the fabulous goldfish that swim around. The personal inscrutability is rescinded for some moments in the love meeting. Body and soul become one, the 'you' and the 'I' become a 'we.' Existence becomes real.

Love also implies a metaphysical leap towards freedom and conviction. The flickering images of reality are fastened to a complete and nuanced picture. Your own body and the other people who up to now had been only boundaries and inhibitions, place one's spirit in a prison cell, become instead windows on the world.

In sensuality, infatuation, and love, human beings are offered a metaphysical provocation, the possibility to enter a new dimension, a new way of life, to leap out into the possibilities that humanity has. This new existence can be called *to be with*, for the loving human being is always first and foremost with the other.

To be with is to understand the dialogic reality of the "You," to experience with all of one's sensuality and intellect that meeting with the other person's pervasive presence. In love, we become lasting to one another; gain consistency and substance, just as old objects with noble qualities are both eternal and transitory. Our common presence becomes something that lasts when we are separated, for that presence has transformed us. In love, the human being is at home, rests with the other with no goal, in peace, lacking narrow minded and egotistical interests.

We are first and foremost a 'You' for the other. *I* am 'we' only in relationship to the "us," in the meeting *with* the other. In these lasting and expansive states of mind, we find a human meeting place of a completely distinct character, literally a new place to be, a new time.

The person is born. Love and freedom, and purpose become living, lasting qualities that transcend the singular being. Thousand means and ways can realize these values, but if our attempts are too little radical, we can kill what should be realized, just as when a human being wants to realize their personality independent of a 'You' and of belonging together. In such a case, the personality will eventually evaporate, for the personality, like a crystal, is shaped from deep human interaction, and made from the honest meeting between the personal in the self and in others.

The spirit of love is not at least to keep holy and universalize the values that make it. The loving human being does not sit in his/her private closet, but instead expresses love directly in being and opinions, to society and their surroundings. Love decentralizes and expands, in loving the one, sympathy and understanding of the many grows.

One can measure the power of owns love in the extended effects it has. It liberates and opens, includes and surrounds ever increasingly an agile and amazing humanity.

Love throws us into the divergent world, into dreams, emotions, poetry, the irrational, and the mystical. The loving human being is suddenly creative.

"When you are falling in love, even the simplest and most commonly endowed human being suddenly has a need to express him or herself in poetry, the language of myth and the divine."[62] Daily life is filled with the blue flowers of love.

The loving person can also be seen as forever tamed by love. The fox says to the little prince: "But if you should want to tame me, my life will be filled with sunshine. I'll know the sound of footsteps that will be different from all the rest. . . .Wheat fields say nothing to me. . . But your hair has the color of gold. So it will be wonderful once you've tamed me. Then the wheat, which also is golden, will remind me of you. And I'll love the sound of the wind that whistles through the wheat fields. . ."[63]

Love can only truly be visible through action. "To verify a thought I have to entrust myself in action by making it my end."[64] "The sole proof of a man lies in his deeds. They are the only irrefutable confirmation of the value of his words and the authenticity of his thoughts."[65]

The Friendly Person

Love tells us that all persons not only have dignity and can love, but are as well thoroughly lovable. Therefore, not only love is the philosophy for the loving human being, but the loving person's world becomes the world of friendship, the living, honest, loving and challenging world of friendship. The person makes generosity and sympathy the basic of human emotions. Sympathy also becomes be the foundation for cognition: our thoughts, ideas, and comprehension. Only when we demonstrate what *Bergson* calls *intellectual sympathy* can we really understand existence.[66]

Friendship is perhaps the most important and universal picture of the loving person. Just as the lie always points to the truth and hate to love, an enemy is an invisible friend. The person concerned just doesn't know it yet. The possibility places intrigue-filled paranoia into a garish light. Why be enemy, when one can be friends?

The unique, the lively, and honest friendship is what the loving human being offers others, an offer of openness, intimacy, and trust.

Mass man offers friendship as uniformity, and it is full of demands to the self and others for adjustment and for unanimity. That is why mass man finds connections only among those who resemble them in their own family and relatives, among those who belong to the same social class and have the same political and ethical points of view. Any eventual problems that suggest any disagreements will result in either a break-up or a strengthened demand for uniformity. The ideal of equality will often be the very foundation for mass man's friendships. Resembling your friends and having friends that resemble you becomes the highest matter of importance in the picture of self and group identity. That others should appear visibly different will be enough to prevent mass man from the risk of becoming closer acquainted with them, even if there is some kind of sympathy. Friendships almost seem to have a function that prevents change and growth; they become more of a protection against the personal than an opening to it. Or friendships become primarily a confirmation of social membership and demonstration of precisely to which group one belongs.

Many gatherings are also dominated by the need for conformity. Those in attendance will be dressed the same, have the same quality clothes, and their behavior will be regulated by conventions in which everyone plays the same role; one, leaves such a party strengthened in one's conviction that one's own group has the best understanding of what is going on in the world.

The *individual* offers friendship that is a competition, a hidden battle over who should admire whom. They feel a constant need to promote themselves both as different from others and more valuable. If mass man is the born twin of everyone and anyone, then the individual is the born pioneer who has a need to come first, be the best, and be remembered the longest.

The individual is endlessly competitive, and often about everything. The most typical competition is about material wealth, but also achievements, grades, distinctions and careers. Other things are less typical, like trying to be the kindest, or the one who most disagrees with the whole world. Or who is the toughest and dares to try the most dangerous or most unpopular actions. Friendships in the sphere of the individual accelerate quickly, the one always trying to pass the other; they drive each other from peak to peak.

The individual's friendships also quickly end; the natural border for the number of possible accomplishments is quickly reached. But some friendships can be lengthy if the one can accept the superiority of the other and one's own inferiority. At the same time, such relationships are threatened; the one in the position of being the superior can grow tired and bored, or the one who is inferior can become rebellious and break out.

Many people, perhaps especially men, are likely to have no friends because they don't want to compete and also can find no basis for friendship in the personal.

Friendship is highly regarded in our society. Many are preoccupied with how to *get* friends. This is often not the real problem, that is, unless it is bullying and malice that cause isolation. The problem is likely part of common attitudes to friendship and a lack of understanding for what it really means to be a friend. Many think that it is a social relationship of exchange, and that one has to have something that others want. This could be parties, food, drinks, favors or social status.

It can be difficult to experience friendship with those kinds of attitudes. You will be unable to develop relationships further than some form of congeniality, hiding the deepest, most personal thoughts from each other. Encounters leave you empty, make you tired, and give you a headache. In that respect, the hangover is an unflattering measure of the content of many friendships. When people want to be friends, without being personal, time spent together, no matter how nice in many ways, can be psychically impoverishing and harm your mental health.

Likely, the problem is that only the very few know how to be a friend in *their own* relationships. It is easy enough to establish ideals for what a friend should be like; it is harder to oneself to develop rules to live by that can realize the friendship.

Being a friend involves using your ability to listen to others, hear what is said and unsaid, to perceive the other as a person, so that the other person can feel that they have been seen. To do this you have to give the relationship time, peace and quiet, and avoid two hazards.

The first hazard is the tendency to privatize. One talks about oneself and one's own stuff, but one listens with a great deal of effort, if the other person do the same. Private problems enter the relationship without any effort to universalize them and give them some importance outside of the solitary life. Like how you always talk about symptoms and incidental phenomena. This is how others necessarily can be shut out of the conversion; you are unable to think yourself out of and the other into a context.

The other danger is quite the opposite and perhaps the most typical for intellectuals. They speak lexically, offering knowledge and references, expressing objectivity, but they never draw on their own private thoughts and lives. They are unable to think themselves into the context, and therefore can never become present enough. In the same way they also shut others out of the communication. The condition for friendship is both to be able to think in yourself and the other at the same time and with the same theme, so that a living and true dialog can emerge.

A friend is someone who offers space to another, and to the relationship between them. Being a friend is giving from your personality to the other so that together you can create something new. A friend meets others with sympathy and shows interest in the experiences that others have had and in their existence. He or she does not ask whether there are any hidden motives but exhibits trust and good feelings for all that the other party reveals about them self. Friends interpret each other goodhearted and express who they are.

Friends gives one another freedom to agree or disagree, generosity is expressed as sincere tolerance. But they help each other only when it becomes necessary and when it means something; they do favors for each other but are careful against disservices.

A friend is neither predictable nor capricious, but like the loving person, tamed. A friend has been civilized out of love for others and for fellowship, has let him/her be led by loving feelings. To be asocial— it is the opposite. This is letting the self be controlled by negative feelings, distrust, ambition, and restlessness. This restlessness translates into flight, break ups, and anxiety for letting the self be imprisoned by love and the relationship, by responsibilities.

The loving person is in friendship in the first person plural. Friendship is a duet; two must be able to swing together to use the language of jazz, spontaneously and in harmony, without having to plan for it to happen. It is life in the relationship itself that *is* friendship, and if it is without life, then it is simply an acquaintance.

Friends understand *each other* and communicate so that they truly share the world when they are together. They move in a common landscape and do not perch on top of their own mountaintops, shouting to one another. The comments of the one can be translated, understood by the other, without using the same words, but with an intuitive understanding of each other's meaning.

Some friends come along spontaneously once you have experienced their wholeness as a person and are yourself experienced that way. Other friendships are created through time, energy, and working at listening and learning, showing warmth and generosity. In many ways, it is easy to be a friend even if friendship occurs only when both parties want it, have interest for it and sympathy for each other.

A world full of friends is a world that is good to live in. While it is impossible to become friends with mass man due to their thick shell of roles, expectations, and façades, and the individual who is an asocial animal refusing to be tamed, the person is a born friend. Friendship is perhaps the one thing the person absolutely can do.

Chapter VIII

Person and Society

USING PERSONALIST PHILOSOPHY AS our support, we can develop a critique of *society*. Our main criticism applies to the few, perhaps even completely lacking possibilities for personal development that our society has to offer each human being.

Whether or not this criticism is taken seriously depends on one's fundamental view of society. If it is the case that every society must necessarily suppress the personal and the person, then this criticism will either be sidelined or wasted. And in many ways, perhaps all societies and communities are shaped by routines, habits, conventions, and the *lack* of individuality and personality. Mass man maintains society on a normal footing, forms groups, and therefore represents order and discipline, seen from without. Perhaps that is how it must be, and the person becomes a rarity who one meets in private life.

Of course, this is not my view. As far as I can determine, the social and the personal are two separate and different dimensions of human existence. The person is something quite different from society's masses and individuals; the personal dimension transcends both of these.

We don't need to imagine that laws and customs that automatically apply to society have consequences for or apply to the person, and vice versa. To the contrary, one can imagine that opposite sets of laws apply to society and to the person. Another possibility that we may be dealing with is two independent, possibly parallel worlds where some characteristics of society affect the person positively and/or negatively, and that a stronger emphasis on the personal would result both in certain positive and negative consequences for society or the separate arena of the private world.

This is my present position; that some kind of indeterminacy exists in the relationship between person and society, between microcosms and macrocosms, and that simultaneously certain conditions in society make it difficult to develop the person, while a number of changes one could imagine would improve this situation. In this chapter, I will concentrate on the obvious attacks on the personal that exist in our society today, while also calling attention to the possibility for positive changes. That this critique of society could have been far more comprehensive and extensive goes without saying. But that will have to wait for another opportunity.

Society's Polar Opposites: the Individual and the Masses

In many ways, a society can be understood as an eternal battle between the individual and the masses. It is first and foremost the masses and the individual who dominate society and its official life, its organizations and institutions. Each in their own way, these phases or types of existence presuppose the impersonal and keep human beings at a distance from each other.

These stages of existence are polar opposites, and sources for conflict. A society that is right in the middle of a conflict between the masses and the individual is doomed to chaos and agonizing, unstable fellowship. This will be the case whether or not the fellowship was formed out of necessity and reality, something that is rare in our welfare state, or was formed through common beliefs and similar opinions.

Our society has an imbalance in the relationship between its large organizations and the individual. To a large degree, it is the large groups, the masses who have the same opinions, who control society. The welfare society is a product of unions, political parties, and organizations. This is overwhelmingly viewed as something positive, considered to be the source of order and justice in society, and protector of the individual. To be able to "get something" on these groups is next to impossible. The stronger an individual is inside the group, the more protected. For example, since the war, doctors have, with no legal authority, deceived children regarding their biological fathers, with no threat of legal action. Anyone who is not part of the medical profession could be sued if they deceived children about their kinship.

The unorganized or the weakly organized individual seems to function as a reason for social problems. These individuals simply won't adjust or are difficult and argumentative. Individuals become criminals, drug addicts, sick and dangerous. These types of individuals are splashed across the first page of the newspapers and become the object of research for social scientists. But at first their crime was only that they would not accept offers from the social groups.

Some individuals receive the opposite treatment; they are admired and cultivated, become celebrities without having achieved anything more than laughing unplanned on a TV screen. Free-spoken individuals will often get a lot of attention, indicating that *free* speech and not the content of the utterance, is the attraction. Daring to stand alone outside of the organized masses inspires admiration, almost no matter how it has been accomplished or what has been said.

From the perspective of organizations, particularly social democracies, the dilemma that follows is often emphasized: Either the individual has to choose safety within the fellowship or loneliness and insecurity in unorganized life. Forcing people to choose between safety at the cost of individuality and an uncertain identity at the cost of security is both like putting a knife to their throat and obscure reality.

This conflict is the first serious obstacle that our society puts in the way of development of the personal. Society, through national, state, and local governments, has completely failed in its responsibility regarding teaching organizations to take any ethical responsibility and teaching the individual how to develop their personality. Society is too one-sided in its preoccupation with power struggles and the irregularity of individuals, too little attentive to their role as teacher and mediator of wisdom and quality of life.

Meta-society

Another substantial obstacle to the development of the personal is what I will term the meta-society, a peculiarity of modern society.

Most of us no longer live *in* a society, but *on top of* one, in the *meta-society*. This means that there are many who are employed to have an opinion *about* society; write, expound and determine things about a society that they stand above or outside.

The responsibility for society does not belong to the people who are actively participating in the society, in the living fellowship, but rather with individuals who are pulled out of society, in meta-groups like politicians, sociologists, therapists, and media. When compared to the time and energy that are used to solve problems in reality, there is probably considerably more energy and time spent to write solutions for the problems of others. The assumption is that problems should be solved on the meta-plane, by people who do not have the problems themselves, but by those who represent those who do have them. That means that they lack contact with the problems and only know of their departmental or organizational history and the theoretically possible solutions. Subsequently, it isn't strange that few problems are solved.

Among other things, the meta-society has made it possible to have a political career without any foundation in a fellowship, and without having any experience in the productive and creative arenas, and even without having appreciable education and life-experience. To settle on politics as your only career is possible because a natural society mainly no longer exits. This society was based on work of vital necessity, on cooperation and solidarity.

The meta-society goes a long way toward explaining why a member of parliament can be recruited from 20-year olds and elected officials can grant themselves increased salaries and benefits while normal citizens have to cut their consumption. Asking politicians to show solidarity is almost pointless, because they do not share reality with the people. Politicians live exclusively in the meta-society, while the people are their work, the objects to be governed. Meta-society has created a new class distinction that is far deeper than anything seen previously. On top are the representatives for all political parties, no matter what their party platform is.

But the main problem that meta-society has created is that it has become more and more difficult to discover what a problem truly is in object-reality, and what is really a meta-problem. The domination of the meta-society makes it seem that meta-problems are far more important than fundamental problems. It seems as though politicians are more preoccupied with creating social programs than with investing in the competence and the time it takes to deal with reality. A well-written bill or regulation seems to be more important than what is actually done.

Meta-society is therefore often simply a window dressing while real society suffers from coincidence, incompetence, and chaos.

When meta-society hides real society, it can be difficult if not impossible to find out what is really going on. People become confused. This confusion also affects their possibility for engagement; what really concerns the individual? If the things that are most important occur on the meta-plane, it is easy for people to pull away and to admit that they just don't know much about the matter or they don't have anything important to say. If so, the nature of the things, as mentioned, lies in its history and its place on the agenda and not in the realties outside of it. And should possibilities for action be removed from the individual, it is quite reasonable to believe that one doesn't have to get involved in the matter; then, one can be released from that uncomfortable feeling of being incapacitated.

The meta-society makes it even more difficult to answer this fundamental question: When am *I* responsible? The answer that the meta-society, encourage is that one is responsible when the problem belongs to the meta-plane, meaning either you are employed to solve the problem, or you represent those who have the problem. When someone has a problem that is close to home, for example you witness a crime, an injustice, a fraud, or whatever, you have to either call in representatives of the meta-society or shut up. Action is forbidden and people must understand that they are without responsibility.

Our strange meta- society can be seen not at least at the fact that we view it as both *reasonable* and natural that people who have problems are not helped by their closest family and friends, but by government offices. This type of public assistance was once an emergency solution to be offered when family or friends did not help or could not. The road to a place in the fellowship today is utmost indirect, people have to be led there and given a map and a compass by the officials in charge.

The meta-plane also shows itself in the type of help that society offers. Government offices also manages human relations, they send an adult here and a child there. But no persons will attach themselves to just anybody, take something from just anybody, or feel something for just anybody. Personal relationships cannot be handed out (justly) in the arena of the public offices. It is extremely unlikely that anyone can gain any valuable personal experiences from any public offices or other checking places.

The meta-society strangles the personal through ensuring that a decreasing number of people have and can live in their own realties and deal with them. But it is still the case that the one who is wearing the shoe knows best where it hurts, and that taking responsibility for your own life is a condition for growth and maturity. The same also applies to becoming a person to the greatest degree possible—it is simply a vital necessity.

That we live in a society of document is not much to do about. But the way the papers or files are written, what they contain, who is allowed to write them and what the consequences are of authoring such papers is impossible to change very much. This presupposes that organizations are willing to take collective responsibility for their actions and that they can be taken to court for assault in the same way as individuals. This also presupposes that meta-society changes its message to citizens and tells them that they can take care of their *own* business, act independently, and take responsibility for their own existence. Then society would be encouraging the development towards the personal.

Public Opinion

Public opinion works alongside of organizations and the meta-society. This opinion is also often shaped by these organizations and meta-society. The goal of public opinion will always be to fortify the power of large groups in society. Our democracy is based on the tacit agreement among these groups on how to balance power among them; that is why public opinion will serve the interests of all of these groups at the expense of the interests of the erratic individuals and persons.

The power of public opinion is largely due to the position of the media as the mouthpiece of the meta-society. The media will necessarily strengthen the power of public opinion.

One obvious reason for this is that the media is under the direct control of the government. Newspapers receive large subsidies and NRK (the Norwegian National Broadcasting Corporation) is a public organ. Those who get their salary from these institutions cannot be unaffected by that fact.

This also means that newspapers can't afford to have a serious falling out with any of the large organizations or the state. This can explain the importance of the single human being to the sale; anyone can afford to have a falling out with a 'nobody' or a badly organized individual. And newspapers need something dramatic to offer every day; they must always take the curiosity of their readers into consideration and their need to be observers of a drama.

The same is true of NRK. A truly serious critique of the state or any of the large organizations and unions would have consequences for NRK's economic structure. This is elementary psychology. And the CEO of the broadcast network is almost always recruited from one of the elite power groups.

The power of NRK lies moreover in the unavoidable structure of this media. Despite the fact that NRK is supported by the government, TV and radio are products. Even the media is just another part of the business world. They have to sell, and they have to sell a lot.

That is why, via NRK, we get a face and a voice, usually a well-dressed and attractive individual, into our living rooms. We need not watch too long before we can decide that we are dealing with a typical salesman. The language is exaggeratedly oral in form, and the smiles are warm. The programs are entertaining and the pictures amazing. For the most part, the media people in NRK, as all other salesmen, give the impression of taking part in our personal reality; media people presented themselves in their programs as our nicest and most entertaining acquaintances. They pretend to exist for us, and do everything to our best. They look us straight in the eyes, speak directly into our ears, the messages are oversimplified and convincing. What more could one wish for?

Now perhaps we should be asking what the TV media are selling? Which products are we are buying? First and foremost, we need to buy the official opinion, faith in the organizations, the unions and the pressure groups; such as each TV personality interprets it. We have to buy the truth that is being served; therefore this attitude of the salesmen.

But we also have to buy the media itself; give the media a meaningful place in our life. The media works hard to be attractive; unless we all spend many hours a day with the media, they are doomed. And can anything be more important than hearing precisely the program on radio or see that program on TV that is being broadcast next week? That is the message from NRK at any rate. While everyone discusses the commercial transmissions at NRK, there is no one who has got hold of how NRK freely goes ahead and advertises for themselves and their own.

The media is one great big commercial. Media personalities advertise their own private tastes, themselves, their scenery, their trips, their books, their music, their art, their culture, their opinions and their perceptions. This becomes clear when you realize just how much time and effort they put into each other; how an NRK journalist seeks out a newspaper journalist and vice versa. All commercials, all propaganda, is in direct conflict with the values of friendship and the person.

The reason for the opposition to commercials on NRK must be viewed as it relates to the public opinions fight against the individual and the private business.

When advertising is used as an advantage for the public economy, for public opinion and the masses, no one has any objections.

The message of the mass media is in complete agreement with the official view of the fellowship. They too define the fellowship as a one-way relationship; it is a place or a gathering where the weak are taken care of. That is why the media tries to occupy culture; culture becomes whatever the media is interested in. Culture comes to the people through the media while in reality it should be the creative persons who teach media what culture is. The media will also always be willing to entertain and help to kill time. The number of programs is completely independent of whether anyone has something important to say or mediate. Simultaneously the media is almost immune from criticism of values. The media will not enter into a dialogue with their public at any price. The exception is those who think that the media does too little for the depersonalizing of society. Therefore, NRK can send more sports but not more culture or socially critical program.

Public opinion is the true power in society. "... one cannot rule against public opinion... power is, when all is said and done, nothing else but a spiritual power."[67] While public opinion pretends to give power to the collective, in reality it gives power to the individuals employed by the media. These individuals are, like others, protected by powerful groups, often outside of the reach of a chain of reactions that may lead a lonely individual to change course. The media are therefore in many ways the clearest model we have for the mass man. They work hard to satisfy anyone as long as it is fully in agreement with public opinion and official fashions.

The role of media in creating public opinion makes the media the power brokers in our society.

This 'executive authority' remains with media because they direct the conversations and the debates of the society. They present, not the things that are good, true or beautiful, but what they think people want and popular viewpoints that will hit home with the public. And to make an attractive offering, media feed mass tendencies; give the people circus (quiz shows, entertainment, revues, comedians, and celebrities, and bread (scapegoats, victims, and crises). Both keep people in place and under the control of the media with its conversations, reflections, and ideals. They fill their mind with daily offers from the media, things that do not often have any intellectual, artistic or knowledgeable standards.

Media also has a close connection to the modern day 'legislative' assembly; pressure groups of all kinds. Pressure groups are masses, anything from three to 500,000 single individuals who believe the same the same thing. People in pressure groups regard any opinion other than their own with horror, dismay and condemnation. Today political parties, organizations, unions, new and old liberation movements give the foundation for public opinion and media willingly harvests from here.

To participate in a pressure group means carrying out meta-actions; strong, organized and "institutionalized" individuals transform themselves into spokespeople for the weak. They will seldom listen to *the real call from the weak*: Let me become one of the strong, give me your place! Let me express my view freely, let me act in my own life and find my personality!

Those who are in "judgment authority" in today's society are again those who arrange and control public opinion: media. Media are at once both executor and judge; the employee comments on a case and gives his/her interpretation. This interpretation and evaluation must naturally be in agreement with public opinion.

Media judges single individuals like groups, and rides on waves of moral indignation and extreme intolerance. Media can never oppose public opinion; media individuals can never attack the media phenomenon itself.

This 'legislative, executive, and judicial' power, thanks to the media, is mass man. It is the masses that form and represent public opinion, and who fight to hold on to power. Individuals are greatly mistaken if they believe that they can fight the masses, no matter whether they belong to a group that is in the majority or a group that is in the minority. Mass man is the strongest. That is why we can state that the majority of Norwegians are defined as a series of weak minority groups.

The intellectual powers that the media and public opinion represent are chiefly the values of the impersonal and distance. Because there maybe is such an enormous difference between the macrocosms and the microcosms, it could happen that society's persons and the living fellowship are going in opposite direction of the public. As long as we do not have a public that is dominated by the values of the person, the direction society is taking will usually end in increased chaos, dissolution, and destruction.

But the conflict between public opinion and the person, as mentioned, is hidden. We could gain some insight if the media were to become a real and true *media*, if they were pure and open intermediaries. What if media personalities were to read their manuscripts with a perfectly normal voice, spoke normally without any actor affectations, avoided entertaining all the time, avoided celebrity for their own sake, lessened the type of editing that constrains the public, and instead found a liberating form, the media could play a healthy role in society. Then people would also perhaps seek out friends and acquaintances and again develop living fellowships in their work lives and their neighborhoods. Only when media is willing to liberate their public can we see what they are truly worth. But if the media were to replace personal reality, they will most likely be successful.

The strength of public opinion is so strong and dominant that we should have a Richter scale so people could be warned that they may unwittingly be moving into a danger zone. But of course, the waves that occur in the mass media when the boundaries are overrun are perhaps good enough. No matter what, there will likely be many in future who speak against the confusion of the meta-society, and the agreements of the large organizations, public opinion and the media's enormous power. The question is whether there will be enough of them and whether they can steer development onto the tracks of the personal. If not, then public opinion will also be the personal's executioner.

Welfare Ideals

There are several more factors in our society that threaten the person and the personal. Ironically, it is our welfare ideas that contribute to the prevention of developing living human relationships.

In Norway (and Scandinavia in general) a welfare society has been constructed; which means a society that is expected to secure all of its inhabitants from want in the form of hunger, housing, and work. It is also expected that citizens use the Department of Social Services, which in the past was known as Poor Relief, whenever necessary. The inability to manage on your own is no longer viewed as an individual, but a collective shame. It is the community that should be ashamed should any of its members suffer any need.

Welfare ideals in themselves are perhaps good enough. The problems are increased wealth. Poverty is not any longer about lacking necessities, but the inability to afford luxury and the unnecessary. The problem is the people who are supposed to use the welfare society.

In the past, people were used to enduring and suffering. They stood meekly with cap in hand, bowing and thanking for the obvious civil rights. Older people still do not make demands. The generations up until the 1950s were used to obeying their parents; child rearing was authoritarian and oppressive. In contrast to this, the welfare society assumed a nurturing role; official employees became parents who would give people what they needed when they needed it. While the people themselves were viewed as unable to act, to want, and to choose, it was assumed that as soon as they were employed at a government office, they were able to act, choose, and want on behalf of others.

The welfare state has in many ways assumed the role for all citizens that parents had in times past, whether these citizens be old or young, helpless or not. Our society is built as a series of compensations in comparison to the generation from the hard thirties and maintains a view of humanity from those days. As a result, the dependent and subdued child is still with us; no longer a child who receives nothing, but a child who demands everything without accomplishing anything, the mass man.

In fact, we view the role of the welfare society as the way to satisfy physical needs and be substantially engaged in the *emotional* needs of people. Childless, healthy young women demand that the state get them pregnant should they be married to a sterile man. Young people without any money demand the ability to be accommodated with both house and children if that is what they want.

The role of the welfare state to care for citizens has become so comprehensive that it also assumes the task of satisfying people's future and imagined needs; everyone's old age is secured, and health care has been transferred to the state. This need to be everyone's mother is so strong that people cannot invest privately in their health. People can naturally use their money on things that damage their health, but they shouldn't save money for an operation that might ease their lives as they age. The welfare state has no strong opposition toward people that make themselves helpless, because their entire justification for existence is based on taking care of helpless people. The more depended people, the more power to the welfare state.

Simultaneously, the welfare state resolves conflicts for its citizens. Just like old-fashioned parents put their children's relationships in order both inside and outside of the family, the welfare state offers a profusion of conflict resolution specialists (and sanctions.) Should any problems arise in relationships between people, they are not expected, and many are unable, to solve them themselves. In come family advisers, sociologists, doctors, nurses, psychologists, psychiatrists, and a series of others like the child protective services, the grievance offices, and the entire legal system. Any private conflict should preferably, and usually is, solved by the government.

This is of course all due to our meta-society, but the welfare ideals help to drive this development in the same direction. Perhaps this is also what has made the meta-society possible.

This is why the welfare state is, in many ways, more dangerous than the older form of the state. Because it promises more, it can do more damage. Perhaps it is the case that the welfare state does give us real help when needed, like reeducation, social security, medical help, grants and cheap loans. But those who do not receive any of those things are worse off than they were in the old days. They do not even have a hand to hold; family and friends disappear when the going gets tough.

And, naturally, the welfare state does not function the way it is supposed to. Anyone who has had any experience with age, sickness, and conflict knows this. When a small portion of the population takes care of the problems for the majority, and simultaneously takes part in the affluence and the welfare, the welfare state becomes impossibility. And it is not money that solves problems. The idea itself of the state as a good mother is an impossibility.

A human being on welfare is a dependent child, a dessert-human being, aware of all that it wants, but not conscious of demands and responsibilities. If a welfare society was a real possibility, and everyone at any time in the state's official offices with their employees had their needs covered, the welfare society would still not result in a living fellowship. A hospital, an institution, a kindergarten or school is a hierarchy, where some are defined as weak and without the ability to decide anything concerning themselves, while others defined as strong.

The ideals of welfare are something *felt*. One feels that everyone should be well off, and therefore, one believes that it is a valid truth. Hedonistic thought is elevated to social law. In reality, people ought to have both good and evil, meet both trials and joys. To live is *also* to suffer, to mourn, to work hard and to lose.

The politicians who drive the welfare state have taken our lives and our choices away from us, make us incubator babies. But politicians shall neither feel for us, nor think, nor act for us. They shall work for us. They shall see to it that buildings, schools, universities, roads and hospitals are erected, their tasks are objects; they shall not give people content of their lives. Naturally, they can care, but they shall not get involved. And they shall try to prevent others from getting involved with the content of people's lives. Their job is of a practical nature; spirit and values are jobs for priests, philosophers, and artists. Not to mention the fact that it is people's own business.

Welfare ideals becomes a threat to the development of the personal because they sweep away relationships *between* people; take away shame and elbowroom, accomplishment, will, and choice from the individual. The rich and plentiful offerings from society make it easy to view the state as a milk cow, and as a result people sacrifice their independence. Simultaneously, the shortcomings of welfare state leave citizens to chaos and coincidence, creating confusion and helplessness.

Ideals of Equality

Another threat to the personal is the ideals of equality on which modern, especially social democratic societies are built.[68] Originally, these ideals were perhaps useful. The deep class-divided society made some citizens pariahs and accepted the fact that a certain number of people by definition could never gain certain benefits, creating a great deal of suffering and destitution. But the ideals of equality in earlier days were concerned with social, economic, and political benefits.

In modern society, again perhaps due to overabundance and wealth, these ideals have been expanded to apply to the human being and not just their benefits. *Human beings* are considered equal: equally good, equally smart, equally talented, and so on. It is only a question of ensuring that the conditions are put in order, and this equality will emerge. If someone achieve more than others, ardent social democrats assume that these achievers have had certain advantages or have been especially good at self-promotion. Or it is believed that they have been unusually diligent and hard working. There are few who believe in the unique, in brilliance, and earth shattering talent, not to mention genius. Genius no longer exists.

Ideals about equality would not be so damaging if they were set high enough. To strive to be equal to a gifted human being, can get one to stretch to new heights, as well as to put oneself into the possibility of a real defeat.

Of course, equality as an ideal has a content, it can be set at a level of the truly gifted, the mediocre, or the dull. To do the latter is unnecessary but with that as a measure, everyone is born equal. To set it at the middle, which is the normal practice, the dull become losers, and the gifted have no need to exert any effort, and just as well conceal their talent as to develop it. They will be rewarded in any case. And despite rewards, they will also become losers if they don't develop what lives inside them. Mass man is created like this. Setting ideals at the best makes many into losers and promotes the individual and uniquely gifted human being. Only when the ideal of equality is set as low as possible, can we avoid having any losers. But we will not have any winners either; art, culture, science, crafts, and society become the biggest losers here. And if the individual can't lose, still the society, the collective can. As previously mentioned, the rules for microcosm do not necessarily apply to macrocosm, and the other way around. And the losses that the collective has to bear can be just as serious and damaging as the ones individuals might experience.

Thus, ideals of equality do not solve any problems. They merely push them onto the collective and make them even more difficult to solve. It is becoming clear that these ideals are absurd and damaging.

The equality that was meant to express human rights in relation to economic and social injustice, and as their duties in relation to God and the value of human life, has become banal and petty with its mechanical interpretation. The masses and their opinions become the priority and the model for existence.

Ideals of equality should only be applied to external phenomena, to objects, benefits and roles; they become dangerous when applied to the human psyche, spirit, and personality.

In this sphere, we have to discuss *equal value*. Equal value is an ethical and personal concept; the same as respect for and recognition of *differences* between human beings. *In spite* of the exceptionality of human beings, they are expected to accept each other for what and who they are. Equal value is based in personal realities; people are deeply different, and this is viewed as a good thing. Simultaneously, it is recognition of the fellowship in human fate. Old age, perhaps sickness, and most certainly death, awaits us all.

Equal value means that we can recognize others as suffering human beings. The fights and the struggles we go through are worth the effort, and therefore worthy of respect. At the end of life, we can all respect each other for having simply lived, and having shown each other that to us life was worth living.

The concept of equal value is well suited to the increase of ethical standards in the interpersonal and inner personal life. It can help us see each other as persons having the same difficulties and the same possibilities, the same rights and the same responsibilities.

Persons vary greatly; each must proceed at his or her own pace, go through his or her own growth, find the way to specific goals, and strive to reach them. There is no debasement when some reach their goals after others, because it is not the same goal. Just as persons are different, so are their goals. Should two people wish to learn the same thing, they will not be able to learn it in the same way, at the same time. Each will have his or her own tempo, each his or her own conditions, interests in the subject and use and enjoyment of it. Each will have his or her own maturation. The goals of persons are unique, and in reality there is no tape at the finish line.

People who believe that they have been robbed of something when they do not have the same benefits or things as everyone else (who do not have them either) are blind to their own personal realities.

Ideals of equality create mass man; to encourage the development of the personal, we have to create the role of the individual. The individual represents the deviant, the different, the dissimilar, and is therefore a condition for the development of equal personal value. The individual walks away from being the same and into being different; but just as one doesn't become a person neither when one is standing alone nor in middle of masses, one doesn't becomes it by just being different. But being different is a condition for developing equal value. To view one who is like you as equal is not any achievement.

Freedom: Communication Realized

Against welfare state, the media, and public opinion have we only personal communication. It is this that strike out on a new course and help us to defeat the obstacles of the society.

In the eternal battle between the individual and the masses, the personal conversation is crystallized. Personal conversation is a pearl created in the battle to promote the very expression that gives life to the person. Against that conversation, public opinion hasn't got a chance because public opinion is truly about nothing, describing what is nonexistent and is simply a conversation about the Emperor's new clothes.

The person is, as mentioned previously, a conversation all its own, an eternal, ongoing conversation at everyone's level and standard, founded in the inner and outer intersubjective experience.

In analytical philosophy, the intersubjective is often understood as something one must settle for when unable to reach a degree of objectivity because of the imperfection of humans. When viewed in this perspective, the intersubjective is viewed as failed objectivity. In the welfare state, controlled as it is by public opinion and ideals of equality, the intersubjective is static; it consists only of the right opinions and changed only from the top down by the strong individuals who control the organizations, lobbyists, and the activists.

In a free society, opinions will also come from below or from outside of the organized and the established. In the real intersubjective the personal is recognized, and the content is dynamic. The intersubjective is recognized just because it expresses the personal and movable. In the true intersubjective a new content will be created by every new person who contributes and for every new conversation that persons conduct with one another.

In contrast to the people who are part of mass opinions, persons are often in disagreement. Disagreements will often be a sign of the personal, but of course is neither a necessity nor a sufficiency. Two persons who express themselves freely and talk about "everything" will steadily experience what we call disagreement. It will concern both small things and big things. But since they do not reduce the conversation to argumentation or bickering, as the individual usually does, they are able to see that disagreement concerns different experiences and different values and different personalities. Therefore, they are able to interchange the one with the other and are enriched instead of feeling threatened. For that matter, it is also possible to claim that persons are almost never in disagreement since disagreement requires the same thing as agreement, the same experiences, the same measuring sticks, the same intensity, but despite all that, different conclusions. The universal understanding of agreement is superficial and simply means that people are not open, while disagreement usually indicates a need for self-promotion. Unanimity and discord act like signals, whether regarding conformity or rebellion, mass man or individual.

True freedom is the ability to express oneself, be heard, and be a contributor to the creation of opinions. True intersubjective means that newcomers are asked about their opinions, and the old unanimity is discussed, new opinions integrated, and together all are able to reach a truer and better agreement than what had previously been done. Clearly, this is all part of an eternal process; new opinions must continually be integrated, and agreements renewed. Nothing is final or adopted; there is no conclusion.

Freedom is the ability to express one's self, to speak up, take part in an act of communication and to get an answer; fellowship is nothing more than living communication.

Just as the psyche and the person are conversations, so is society. It is the conversation, the debate, created in a real intersubjective togetherness that creates society and a fellowship. Our society is our conversation, our common values are the rules we follow, the way we talk to each other, and what results are reached or not reached. Our history is a survey of all of our agreements. All society between people is formed from the conversation between them and the quality of that conversation.

In the absence of the conversation, the real dialog, and the living communication, there can be no real society. There is only a collection of people with no contact with others or even with themselves. If you want to know what kind of society we live in, write down the public debates and the patterns of the conversations that you usually participate in. There is where you will find our fellowship, our life together, our values. As a comparison, we can make a list of the topics, the values, the experiences you believe are fundamental in a personal life and unconditional ethical goodness. If there is a great discrepancy, then that means the fellowship you believe is present, is just an empty shell.

Personal Society

Each human being is faced with the same problem: How to find a niche, one that is big enough for one to express oneself as a person, and small enough so that other persons gain vital meaning? The niche one is searching for must be able to contain the entire self, while at the same time not close one off. Personal wholeness must be expressed both in relation to oneself and the surroundings.

The danger of the person is to become self-sufficient and thereby reduced to an individual or insufficient and thereby reduced to a mass man. Let me repeat: the shape of the personal is communication. The communication skills depend on the attention one give to oneself and others, ones training to listen on many levels and planes at the same time, and the ability to see the interaction in a realistic whole.

If society's institutions and organizations are to serve the person, they must adapt to this fundamental shape and rhythm. To create a personal society, we have first and foremost to work on our routines for communication and our communication systems. There are many simple methods that can create flow in the dialog and in the communication systems.

One important method is *transparence*: the people who are actually the active parts of the communication systems have to be named. It is not the political parties, the unions, and the newspapers that have opinions. It is always the boards, the committees, the councils and the commissions who have opinions. Institutions and organizations cannot believe anything. These are nothing more than names for a collection of individuals. The anonymous majority opinions presented to us are expressions of tactical supports for an organization, institution or leader.

In a personal society we would always have the right to know the names of those who are behind and responsible for the expressed opinions no matter how popular and universal they may be. If this requires time so they can all be named, then we need to take that time. Politicians should share public opinion amongst themselves. Some should take responsibility for that opinion. Perhaps that would force them to think through their resolutions. Who would for example take personal responsibility for the children who are taken from their biological fathers as anonymous sperm donors?

The tendency of institutions, organizations, and the media to make those who are actually responsible into some anonymous being, will confuse, suppress and control communication. Who among us feels able to oppose a particular political party? Not to mention labor unions. And should you attempt that, with whom should you speak? Who will listen to what you are saying? Their anonymity makes them impregnable and depersonalizing.

Naturally, the fact that institutions and organizations take on a kind of personal life is complicated. We form impressions of large and small groups that impact us with a positive or negative force, and we are happy to express ourselves about them. Despite this, it is always the single person who means.

For this reason, the most important question in communication between persons and social systems is, as in all other situations, to inquire just who the sender is, and what kind of human being the sender is. WHO IS TALKING? WHO MEANS? Does the sender live in the characterless, egotistical individual's world or the life of the dialogue in the personal? In order to communicate we have to have a face and a pair of eyes to look into. No one can communicate with anonymous pronouncements, even if you can believe that you understand what they might imply.

Pure information is a completely different prospect. When the Transportation Secretary gives us information about bad roads it is usually unnecessary to know who the secretary is. An exception would be if the secretary is mad, evil or a military enemy. On the other hand, the message would likely have reached many more people if the secretary's name were known. A well-known person who works with transportation issues has a better chance of being heard than any anonymous Emergency Services do.

Big institutions and organizations rarely deliver pure information. They deliver messages that people should pay attention to. That is why the names of those who speak on behalf of a group should always be available. Those who are responsible for fundamental issues should be well known. Strong and powerful individuals hide in anonymity.

This is especially important in the world of party politics. Our political system is expensive. We have a representative democracy, not a democracy of persons. It is vulnerable to injustice and tyranny. Politicians are not elected because of their strong ethics.

Our goal should be a democracy controlled by persons. Those who run for public office should be elected based on their personal qualities and well known to us.

If it is the case that we have an impotent political system, then we will need to sit down and rethink democracy. Representational democracy is not necessarily the final answer to the distribution of power in society. That it was the right answer two hundred years ago does not mean that it is the right answer today. Our political systems should be processes. Not at least one should consider the possibility that the democratization process may have a natural limit: namely, the competence and insight of the individuals. What people have no idea, or competence about, they should not have power to decide about. Such a limit in the democratizing processes has already been accepted if not expressed. One does not elect children, mentally handicapped, or mentally sick people into political institutions because they have a right to representation from one of their own. That also adult, normal people have limits is just as obvious.

Alongside of the systematic analyzing of institutions, organizations, political, and cultural information systems including the media, by the shaping of minds through open dialog at all levels and in all cases, society needs to welcome *critique*. Critique isn't something that one rejects, or answers once and for all, critique is something one has to live with; it is a major part of the intersubjective process.

But most people in the centers of power try to live outside of or independent of critique. They suppress it in themselves and others in any situation where power is present, power in the form of personal gain, forceful bosses, the anonymous, the conventional others or public opinion. This explains a strange phenomenon that many experience quite often; people are mostly inclined to be critical of others when they meet them in corridors or are alone with them. As soon as they sit in a meeting, they go along with resolutions and neglect their own critical position.

Critique seems to thrive best in the darkness of privacy. When it becomes clearly visible, attitudes of the majority do change. If critique comes from the outside, it is viewed as either a misunderstanding or as unfounded, and even likely due to a lack of knowledge. If it comes from the inside, it is regarded as not being solidarity.

But criticism should come from both the inside and outside. External critique tells us something about the other group's experiences, and they have a right to express their opinions. Internal criticism is far more important. Individuals inside the centers of power have a *responsibility to criticize*. Living with critique means just that. People will only dare to live a life like this when they value the personal. Only persons dare have an opinion.

Critique is the flip side of the "right" point of view, the footnotes and the commentaries, the complementary and the negative. It creates connections and totality.

As a next step, we need to work on creating processes that are not controlled, but help shape dialog and could work towards *reconciliation* between groups. It is chiefly the mass media that should be responsible for these processes. Things must be analyzed as a whole.

Meetings of this type will have no resemblance to the usual debates on TV in which a moderator tries to prevail over as many participants as possible at the same time and where the participants all talk about their own causes.

Reconciliation is more about insight and knowledge and understanding than about balance and tolerance. The problem with the mass-dominated and individualist dominated societies is that there is a lack of profound wisdom, empathy, intimate understanding, and personal experience. The superficial and the chaotic, along with massive whining and complaining, destroy the processes of communication in society.

The *processes of negotiation* are different from the processes of reconciliation and are just as important. There is much that we cannot reconcile ourselves to or get others to understand. The feeling of having a possibility to attain something with opponents will help to better communication in society, both because it adds some degree of safety to know that the distance between us is not something we can't overcome, and it offers hope.

But a process of this sort requires maturity; it is necessary to understand that existence is not some idyllic place where no one is ever hurt, or treated unjustly, or is never discriminated against.

Our society has no lack of hate and places for revenge. We have a justice system, police, prison, institutions, and countless way to sanction people and groups who are our or society's opponents.

What society is lacking is a place for *mediation*. These may be the meeting places that society could be part of and planning. But they could just as well be established through private initiative. The whole point of these places must be that they have no sanctions in their back pockets and that they do not practice therapy. It is neither punishment nor treatment that is needed.

The contrasts between punishment and therapy often exclude other possibilities. The sick and criminal are the ones who most need to develop the ability to reconcile and to negotiate with the society against which they have struggled. Most of them have a need to be able to constantly talk themselves back into a connection, participate in communication, understand more, and experience deeper.

Such places to meet can be quite natural: the café table, shops and streetcar stops. But due to the complete lack of understanding Norwegian politicians have for the need for cheap cafés and a good means of public transportation, these have naturally become unusual. It is ironic how social democrats have created as society full of distance between people.

Society lacks people with a broader perspective who can reconcile and negotiate, heal and make whole. Society lacks people who are in a relationship of friendship to their entire society.

The personal society should become a society where friendship is a dimension of all relationships. It is also thinkable that friendships could be *the* foundation for all relationships. At any rate is it possible and realistic that far more people than is the case today could base their relationships to others on the value of the person and friendships. Friendly attitudes cost very little and are more fruitful for being and acting together.

A Society of Persons: Meaningfulness

In this chapter I have given a short and general critique of society. Much more could have been said, but I do not believe that it is a critique of society that is most pressing. This is because society can overwhelmingly be considered as something distant or absent. Decisions and centralized processes reach us in daily life like drips. And society does not feel shame or think morally. Only persons can do that.

This is why it is far more important to increase our attention to the sphere of the personal. Everyone can do something on a personal level. No one can do everything, but everyone has something that they can do. We can't make any general laws or rules; we must all find our way from our own unique platform and act as ethically creative as possible.

Through the personal we can imagine the possibility of contributing to a better world. It is not certain, but the possibility is there. The relationship between the social macrocosms and the personal microcosms is as mentioned indeterminate; but this does not mean that our actions don't have consequences in a greater context. As society exists today, the person and society seem to be on a collision course. A reason for this could be that we no longer recognize the microcosm as something distinct and are not willing to act inside the dimensions that determine. If the personal development lacks consequences for society, the macrocosm, it can even though be of importance to individual human beings and their networks. And that is no small thing.

A society of persons is nothing more than a society where people truly communicate and have a living and fruitful dialog with each other. Without the personal, everything of value and quality will collapse. It is only the personal that embraces the fellowship, and keeps it together, gives it meaning.

Therefore, a society of persons is a place where everyone can seek meaning and have a reasonable chance at finding it. The degree of meaningfulness tells us something about the quality of both our little society and the big one. The big is also always small; it is nothing more than relationships from person to person standing in a row, hands holding on to each other creating the living society. The more broken relationships, the worse, the emptier, and the more lifeless society will be.

Only the fewest are willing to join hands and hold hands. In Norwegian society many are yelling that the wolf is coming, but no one believes the other, and no one helps unless they are paid to do so. That paid help will never do much good because it is never personal and was never meant to be personal. Love from a prostitute, interest and friendship from a sociologist or psychologist, all is forced, and usually superficial, artificial and inauthentic. But if real feelings have been deceived often enough, no one will be able to tell the difference.

To create a meaningful society, we have to start a crusade against public opinion, the prized consensus, and all mass opinions. When people stand together because of their agreements of opinion, when opinions and views are the fundamental reasons for the group, then intolerance is on its way into the group. For persons, as mentioned, do not often agree, not on one thing or on all things, or even on most things. Persons disagree, or at least believe that they do. They have different perspectives on the world, different experiences and different assessments.

We can also work to give art and culture a far broader and more important place in daily life. There are dimensions that good and valuable art and culture offer, which work as healing and give meaning.

Many berate today's youth and even adults for their lack of knowledge about history. But that is simply one symptom of a general lack of culture, a lack of understanding of the whole that binds people to each other and to reality. Living without traditions or experiences with values expressed and shaped inside the universal and eternal art forms, abandons people to chaos and confusion. Lack of substance derives from lack of relationship to the timeless, from lack of interest and respect for anything that is not private and coincidental.

And we can give philosophy a far more central place in all forms of education, possibly even in elementary education. *Leo Tolstoy* once said that five-year old children were the greatest philosophers. The wondering and open thought finds connections and offers the human beings a place in something that is greater than they. Simultaneously it develops respect for humanity; all wisdom comes from people themselves, even if some are wiser than others. Learning to respect humanity is impossible if one seldom or never relates to the best of what people have created and brought forth, and never has any real knowledge about what human beings are capable of.

Sociologists and social scientists see us only as representatives for the groups to which we belong, and they are far too dominant in forming public opinion. Their view of human beings is so focused on roles that it does not present us with the richness that can be found in each person and in the loving human being. Society does not need more rationalizing experts and economists, but more experts in communication and people with the ability to personalize ideas, feelings, thoughts, actions and values.

The true understanding of humanity will always be expressed best in art, culture and philosophy, with the great artists and philosophers. Both art and philosophy can teach us to think judiciously about totalities grounded in reality. Both help us to search for the real living meaning, and to recognize it when we meet it. For wealth is wealth in personality and in spiritual values, wealth in friends and meaning.

Recommended Literature

Scandinavian

Buber, Martin, Jeg og Du, Kbh. 1964
Kierkegaard, Søren, Collected Works, b. 1–20, Kbh. 1962

English

Knudson, Albert C, The Philosophy of Personalism, NY. 1969
Macmurray, John, The Form of the Personal, London 1961
Macmurray, John, Freedom in the Modern World, 1968
Macmurray, John, Reason and Emotion, 1962

French

Lacroix, Jean, Le Personalisme, Lyon, 1981
Mounier, Emmanuel, Oeuvres de Mounier, Paris 1961
Nédoncelle, Maurice, Explorations Personnalistes, Paris, 1970
Nédoncelle, Maurice, Personne Humaine et Nature, Paris, 1962

Chapter Endnotes

1. Marcel Mauss: *A category of the human mind* in *The category of the person*, ed. Michael Carrithers, Steven Collins, Steven Lukes (Cambridge, Cambridge University Press, 1985), 22.
2. Norwegian dictionary of synonyms, Kunnskapsforlaget, 1984, Oslo.
3. José Ortega y Gasset, *Massenes oprør* (Oslo, Gyldendal norsk forlag, 1934) 14–15.
4. Ortega y Gasset, *Massenes oprør,* 13–14.
5. Emmanuel Mounier, *Personalism* (London, University of Notre Dame, 1952) 117.
6. Marianne Fredriksson and Britta Hansson: *Kjærlek, jämnlikhet og ekteskap?* (Stockholm, Wahlstrøm &Widstrand, 1975) chapter 8.
7. Elias Canetti, *Crowds and Power* (New York, Farrar, Strauss and Giroux, 1984), 258.
8. Canetti, *Crowds and power,* 259.
9. Nina Karin Monsen: *Fra den opprørske til den totalitære bevissthet* (Oslo, Morgenbladets Månedsmagazin), 30/1–87.
10. Canetti, *Crowds and power,* 382.
11. Nina Karin Monsen, *Jomfru, mor, eller menneske? Feministisk filosofi* (Oslo, Universitetsforlaget, 1984) 117—118.
12. John Macmurray, *Freedom in the Modern World* (London, Faber and Faber, 1968), 156.
13. Mounier, *Personalism,* 92.
14. Mounier, *Personalism,* 11.
15. Ernst Becker *The Denial of Death* (New York, Free Press, 1973) see chapter 10.
16. Martin Buber: *Jeg og Du* (Copenhagen, Munksgårdsserien, 1964),(*I and Thou*; Edinburg, T&T Clark, 1994).
17. Rene Descartes: *Discourse on Method* (London, The Whitefriars Press, Penguin Classics, 1960) 61.
18. Nina Karin Monsen: *Jomfru, Mor, eller Menneske,* 14–15.
19. Hermann Hesse: *Siddhartha* (Oslo, Gyldendal, 1976) 97.
20. Emilia Fogelklou: *Barhuvad* (Stockholm, Bonnier, 1951), 53.
21. Ortega y Gasset: *Massenes oprør,* 56.
22. From Bernardo Villarrazo: *Miguel de Unamuno: glosa de una vida.* (Barcelona, Aedos, 1958) 179–80.
23. Ortega y Gasset, *Massenes oprør,* 146.
24. Francesco Alberoni: *Vennskap* (Oslo, Det norske samlaget, 1968).
25. John Macmurray, *The Self as Agent* (London, Faber & Faber, 1969), 76.
26. Bruno Bettelheim, *The Empty Fortress* (New York, The Free Press, 1972), 233–43.
27. Macmurray, *Freedom in the Modern World,* 55.

Chapter Endnotes 139

28. Fritjof Capra: *The Tao of Physics* (London, Fontana,1975).
29. Michael Polanyi, *Personal Knowledge* (London Routledge and Kegan Paul, 1957).
30. Carl Rogers, *On Becoming a Person* (Boston, Houghton Mifflin, 1961) 25.
31. Peter L. Berger, *A Rumor of Angels* (New York, Doubleday & Company,1970).
32. Abraham Maslow, *The Farther Reaches of Human Nature* (London, A Pelican book, 1971) 125.
33. Carl Jung, *Jeget og det ubevisste* (Oslo, Cappelen, 1985) 122.
34. Polanyi, *Personal knowledge*.
35. Macmurray, *The Self as Agent*, 74.
36. Mounier, *Personalism,* 38.
37. See Sigmund Freud's theory of personality.
38. John Locke (1632-1704) maintained that a newborn human being had an empty consciousness, a tabula rasa.
39. Max Stirner, *The Ego and His Own* (New York, Harper Torchbooks, 1971) 49.
40. Martin Heidegger: *Sein und Zeit* (Tübingen, Max Niemeyer Verlag, 12. ed. 1972) 4th chapter, § 4.
41. Kierkegaard, *Begrepet Angst, Samlede Verker* (Copenhagen, Gyldendal, b.3.3.ed.1962) 153.
42. Mounier, *Personalism,* 41.
43. This is often ascribed to Socrates (470-399 b. Kr.).
44. Helm Stierlin, *Konflikt og forsoning* (Oslo, Fakkelbok 1974), 47.
45. Stierlin, *Konflikt og forsoning,* Chapter 3.
46. Gregory Bateson, *The Cybernetics of "Self," A theory of alcoholism*, in *Steps to an ecology of mind* (London, Paladin, 1973).
47. Carl Rogers, *Person to Person (*New York, Real People Press, Lafayette 1967).
48. This is usually called the categorical imperative; if an action is good, it should be made a universal law.
49. Henri Bergson, *Tiden och den fria viljen,*(Stockholm,Wahlstrøm & Widstrand, 1912).
50. Oscar Magnusson, *Jeg Vil Leve* (Oslo, Gyldendal, 1967)162.
51. Magnusson, *Jeg Vil Leve,* 162.
52. Jens Bertelsen, *Individuation* (Copenhagen, Borgen Forlag, 1975).
53. Simone de Beauvoir, *Eksistensialismen og den borgerlige snusfornuft* (Oslo, Cappelens Upopulære, 1968).
54. Nina Karin Monsen, "Sentralt i nazismen: Okkultisme, døden og ren livmorfilosofi," *Morgenbladets Månedsmagazin,* May 4, May 7—9, 1984.
55. Wilhelm Grønbech: *Friedrich von Schlegel i årene 1771-1808*, Copenhagen (Levin og Munksgard,1935) 8-17
56. Francesco Alberoni, *Forelsking og kjærleik* (Oslo, Det norske samlaget, 1983).
57. Alice Miller, *Det sjalvutplånade barnet, og søkande etter en äkta identitet* (Stockholm, Wahlstrøm & Widstrand, 1981).
58. Nina Karin Monsen, "*Erotikk og frihet*," *Morgenbladets Månedsmagasin,*(April 30, 1987)
59. Bertram Dybvad Brochman: *Fandens efterladte papirer,* Bergen, Det frie samfunds forlag, 1934) 103.
60. Danish psychology couple who had a column in the newspaper *Dagbladet* in the 1970s.
61. Wilhelm Reich, *The Function of the Orgasm* (London, Panther book, 1970).
62. Alberoni, *Forelsking og kjærleik*.
63. Antoine de Saint-Exupéry, *Den lille prinsen* (Copenhagen, Jespersen og Pio, 1970), 60.

64. Macmurray, *The Self as Agent*, 202.
65. Mounier, *The Character of Man* (London, Rockliffe,1956) 122.
66. Henri Bergson, *The Creative Mind* (New York, Citadel Press, 1946).
67. Ortega y Gasset, *Massenes oprør,*120.
68. "Social-democracy" is used here with an expanding meaning, on the ground that social-democratic thinking is common in all political circles.

www.ingramcontent.com/pod-product-compliance
Lightning Source LLC
Chambersburg PA
CBHW050826160426
43192CB00010B/1912